CONTENT STRATEGY

FOR THE WEB

— SECOND EDITION —————————————

KRISTINA HALVORSON
MELISSA RACH

Foreword by Sarah Cancilla, Facebook

Content Strategy for the Web, Second Edition

Kristina Halvorson and Melissa Rach

New Riders

Find us on the Web at: www.newriders.com
To report errors, please send a note to errata@peachpit.com

New Riders is an imprint of Peachpit, a division of Pearson Education.

Copyright © 2012 by Kristina Halvorson and Melissa Rach

Project Editor: Michael J. Nolan
Development Editors: Tenessa Gemelke and Margaret Anderson
Production Editor: Cory Borman
Copyeditor: Gretchen Dykstra
Proofreader: Rose Weisburd
Interior Design and Composition: Kim Scott, Bumpy Design
Cover Designer: Sean Tubridy
Indexer: Joy Dean Lee

ISBN 13: 978-0-321-80830-1
ISBN 10: 0-321-80830-4

15 2020

Printed and bound in the United States of America

ADVANCE PRAISE FOR *CONTENT STRATEGY FOR THE WEB, SECOND EDITION*:

"The first edition of Kristina Halvorson's little book was like a rip in the Matrix through which light poured. In the space of a few chapters, she had changed our field forever, for the better. This second edition retains all that was wonderful in the first book, while yielding dazzling new insights into the hows and whys of content strategy."

— Jeffrey Zeldman, author, *Designing With Web Standards*

"When I wanted to introduce content strategy as a 'must' for eBay Europe, I bought a copy of *Content Strategy for the Web* for everyone I needed to influence. Two years and a content strategy team later, it clearly worked! By far the most comprehensive and accessible book on content strategy available. Required reading for our entire team."

— Lucie Hyde, Head of Content, eBay Europe

"*Content Strategy for the Web* is the most important thing to happen to user experience design in years."

— Peter Morville, author, *Information Architecture for the World Wide Web* and *Ambient Findability*

"Marketers, take note: From mobile and social media to email and websites, killer content is central to your online success—but without a solid, centralized content strategy, you're doomed from the start. Like no other book, *Content Strategy for the Web* gives you the tools you need to get the right content to the right people in the right place at the right time. Essential reading for marketers everywhere."

— Ann Handley, CMO, MarketingProfs and author, *Content Rules*

"This is the go-to handbook for creating an effective content strategy. The Post-It® notes and dog-eared pages in my copy are evidence of that!"

— Aaron Watkins, Director of Digital Strategy, Johns Hopkins Medicine

"Kristina Halvorson and her company, Brain Traffic, are central to the emerging discipline of content strategy."

— James Mathewson, Search Strategy and Expertise Lead, IBM

"*Content Strategy for the Web* touched off the explosive growth of content strategy and its recognition as a critical field of practice. Amazingly, this second edition doesn't just keep up: it pushes content strategy in a more mature—and valuable—direction."
 — Louis Rosenfeld, author, *Information Architecture for the World Wide Web* and *Search Analytics for Your Site*

"Kristina Halvorson is a force to be reckoned with. In three short years, she has single-handedly brought content strategy to the forefront of the UX community's attention. I'm in awe of how quickly she's mobilized a small army of content strategists, and can't wait to see where she goes next."
 — Jared Spool, CEO and Founding Principal, User Interface Engineering

"This little red book is responsible for changing the way I think about designing for the Web, and I don't think I'm alone. After a decade of treating content like an after-thought, *Content Strategy for the Web* helped us fix our priorities, and gave us a better way forward."
 — Ethan Marcotte, author, *Responsive Web Design*

"The web isn't about only your website anymore. What does that mean for your content strategy? Kristina and Melissa answer with sassy and sound advice."
 — Colleen Jones, author, *Clout: The Art and Science of Influential Web Content*

"If the loss of potential customers and brand degradation keep you up at night, good. There may not be monsters under your bed, but they're in your web presence—and they're coming to get you. *Content Strategy for the Web* offers practical, effective tech-niques to keep the monsters at bay, whether you're waging war in a small business or on behalf of a corporate behemoth. Scared? Not anymore."
 — Margot Bloomstein, Principal, Appropriate, Inc. and author, *Content Strategy at Work*

"If you want your organization or your clients to be successful online, you need to help them think—and act—strategically about all their content. You need this book."
 — Janice (Ginny) Redish, author, *Letting Go of the Words: Writing Web Content that Works*

For the staff at Brain Traffic, whose hard work, brave insights,
and shared sense of humor inspired every page that follows … again.

And for our families, whose loving patience and
support made this book possible.

"The best people are the ones that understand content. They're a pain in the butt to manage, but you put up with it because they are so good."

— Steve Jobs

CONTENTS

STRATEGY

SUCCESS

FOREWORD

· ·

THE RAPID RISE OF CONTENT STRATEGY AT FACEBOOK AND BEYOND

At Facebook, employees are empowered to be bold in the name of innovation. "Move Fast and Break Things," "What Would You Do If You Weren't Afraid?" and "Done Is Better Than Perfect" are a few of the mottos pasted on the walls at Facebook headquarters.

Back in 2009, Facebook content was getting "done," but it was far from perfect. Engineers, designers and product managers were writing most of the copy. If you had a keyboard, you were a copywriter. If you could commit code, you were a publisher. And there was a lot of content: menus, navigation text, product tours, multi-step forms, nomenclature, in-product education, help pages, blog posts, and much more. Less-than-perfect content meant confused and frustrated users, and it was taking its toll on the brand.

The Facebook Design and User Experience team decided it was time to create a new role within the department. They called it "content strategist."

Just a few weeks before the job posting went up, the first edition of *Content Strategy for the Web* was published. Soon after, the Facebook team contacted author Kristina Halvorson for advice about the position, and she graciously offered suggestions about what to say in the posting and where to look for candidates. She also helped get the word out.

I'd been working as a content strategist at eBay for several years when I spotted Kristina's reference to the job posting. I tucked my already well-worn copy of Kristina's book under my arm and headed off to interview at Facebook. They hired me.

***

Soon after I started at Facebook, I discovered that most of my new coworkers thought "content strategist" was a highfalutin term for "copy editor." They filled my inbox with questions like, "Is there a better word for this?" and "Should the period go inside or outside the quotation mark?" I even had an engineer free-type my rough copy ideas directly into the code for the live site. Thrilling, yes, but not exactly the methodical, holistic process I was hoping for.

I needed to find a way to introduce real content strategy into a system that was hardwired to reject anything that might gunk up the works. In the past, I might have organized a meet-n-greet/dog-and-pony/brown-bag extravaganza to educate to my colleagues about the benefits of content strategy. But my usual approach wasn't going to fly at a company that valued action far above talk. Instead, I heeded the "move fast" writing on the walls and focused on gaining quick wins.

I first set my sights on a group of links in the lower corner of the Facebook homepage. These links offered people the chance to invite friends to Facebook, connect with friends already there, and try Facebook Mobile. The links didn't drive a lot of traffic and weren't an important piece of the team's strategy, so they didn't want to dedicate resources to improving them. But I was welcome to change the copy. So I did, relying completely on my content strategy intuition to guide my decisions (there was no time for testing, after all). At the very least, I knew I could make the calls to action clearer and more compelling.

Mere hours after I made my quick-and-dirty changes, we rolled out the new version of the content module. The result? Net traffic to this area of the page rose 56%. Which is to say, *six million more people* found friends, invited friends, and tried Facebook Mobile every week, purely as a result of those tiny improvements.

Over the next few months, I gained a few more quick wins for content. And each time I tackled a project or fulfilled a request, I carefully framed my proposals in the context of the larger Facebook content strategy that was beginning to evolve. I also tailored my recommendations to the audience at hand: When working with engineers, I tried to make things simple and empirical, often relying on spreadsheets and "if-then" statements. With designers, I went visual. And with executive stakeholders, I always made an effort to reference bigger-picture goals.

When someone championed the cause of content strategy, that person became a "FOCS" (friend of content strategy), and was awarded a coveted FOCS tee. As in, "You know that guy Matt? He's a total FOCS."

Soon, people started to solicit my help on more complex problems. Questions about tone, structure and site-wide consistency began to outnumber those about grammar and syntax. The company began giving enthusiastic support (and budget) for longer-term, content-driven initiatives.

Today, a mere two years later, there are nine content strategists on the Facebook team, and we hope to welcome several more by the end of 2012. We work alongside product managers, designers, engineers, and user researchers on every major product launch. We've developed a comprehensive set of content standards for the company. And we serve as a hub for the teams throughout Facebook that touch user-facing content, including product marketing, user operations, and the lawyers.

***

In the two years since I started at Facebook and *Content Strategy for the Web* first came out, the discipline has come into its own. Meetup groups have formed all over the world. People are gathering at conferences dedicated exclusively to content. Not unlike Facebook itself, content strategy has spun into a spirited community of people who are excited to share new ideas and perspectives—allowing the discipline to advance at an amazing clip.

Content Strategy for the Web has played a huge role in educating web practitioners and business leaders about why good content matters. Not only does the book champion a strategic approach to content, it also demystifies how to do it. Whether you're a seasoned content strategist or it's your first time at the rodeo, you've got everything you need to create, deliver, and govern useful, usable content right here.

**

Facebook's culture is unique, but what moved the cause of content strategy forward here could happen anywhere—including where you work.

- **Demonstrate value on your own terms.** Be proactive, and identify tiny projects that will showcase the benefits of content strategy. Then get them done, with or without resources.

- **Apply content strategy to your content strategy.** Frame each recommendation and each success within the context of the larger content strategy, even if the request was tactical in nature. And do it in a way that will appeal to your audience.

- **Friend everyone.** Cultivate allies, find your FOCSes, and make them T-shirts.

In 2009, the content strategy community was small. Now it's vast, and eager to support you in your efforts to make a better web through better content. Today, when you tell people you're a content strategist, the question is no longer, "What's content strategy?" Now it's, "When can you start?"

Join us as we move toward a web where content strategy is not simply nice to have, but an essential part of what we make and imagine.

Sarah Cancilla
Content Strategist, Facebook

BEFORE WE BEGIN...

• •

If you're reading this book for the first time, then hello! It's lovely to meet you. And if you're familiar with the first edition, then hey, welcome back. Glad to see you again. Give us a hug.

So. Things out there in the world of content strategy have changed pretty significantly since the first edition of *Content Strategy for the Web* was published. What used to be a niche topic discussed by only a few hardcore content nerds has become a worldwide movement in organizations of all shapes and sizes. Hooray! More hugs all around.

As the conversation continues to gain momentum, the field of content strategy is evolving at lightning speed. And so, by necessity, this second edition of *Content Strategy for the Web* is a much different book from the first. But don't worry. All new material has evolved directly from the methodology described in the first edition; all revisions are based on the shared knowledge of the wider content strategy community, and our own experiences at Brain Traffic, our Minneapolis-based content strategy firm.

And now, a few things to note:

WHAT THIS BOOK IS

This book is an introduction to the practice of content strategy. It describes some of the key benefits, roles, activities, and deliverables associated with content strategy.

We wrote this book for people who want to understand what content strategy is, why it's important, and how to go about getting it done.

This book also makes the case for content strategy as a legitimate, necessary practice in any and all organizations that create and publish content online.

Throughout the book, we describe processes and methodologies that may be applied to all kinds of content (not only text). And as you read, remember that just about everything we write about can be scaled and tailored to fit your needs.

WHAT THIS BOOK IS NOT

This book is not The Complete Guide to Everything You Ever Need to Know About Content Strategy, Ever.

We hope you find this book a valuable reference tool for a long time to come, but don't mistake it as the only book you'll ever need. In fact, here are a few specific topics this book intentionally does not cover (at all, or in detail):

- Content management systems (CMS) strategy (software selection, design, and implementation)
- Translation and localization
- Personalization and behavioral targeting
- Content marketing
- Social media planning
- Metadata strategy
- SEO
- Reuse and structured content (or "intelligent content")
- Single-channel strategy (e.g., mobile)

Yes, a content strategist will often assume responsibility for the activities and deliverables associated with each of these. In many cases, there are already several solid resources available about these practices, both online and offline. We're keeping our focus on an introduction to content strategy, so we've made it our job to synthesize this information and frame it up in ways that allow teams to tackle content challenges holistically.

WHAT'S NEW IN THIS EDITION

When you set out to write a second edition, it's awfully tempting to scrap everything and write an entirely different book. Instead, we've tried to strike a balance: plenty of new information for readers of the first edition, but a similar introductory flavor for our first-time readers.

As the proud owner of this shiny new edition, here's what you'll get:

- Expanded and restructured processes and tools for the research, development, and implementation phases of content strategy
- Recent case studies examining the impact content strategy has had on a variety of small and large organizations
- An examination of the ways content-focused disciplines and job roles work together
- Discussion of the roadblocks you may encounter and ways the field of content strategy continues to evolve

A NOTE ABOUT CONTENT STRATEGY FOR THE "WEB"

Content strategy. It's not just for websites anymore.

Actually, content strategy was *never* just for websites. In fact, it's been around a lot longer than the web. So why all the recent attention?

While organizations have struggled for decades—centuries, even—to make sense of their content, they were always able to keep the chaos (and the consequences) to themselves. Then came websites, which created the perfect content strategy storm. Suddenly, organizations had to put all of their content (product info, investor reports, press releases, etc., etc.) in one place. For the first time. For all the world to see. And, it hurt.

You can redesign a home page. You can buy a new CMS. But unless you treat your content with strategic consideration, you can't fix your website. Once people started to accept this fact, the conversation took off. It's a pain point everyone shares, and content strategy offers relief.

Here's the other thing: In our opinion, focusing on the web is still the easiest way to learn about content strategy. **Once you "get" content strategy for the web, you can easily see its applications across platforms and throughout the enterprise.**

All that said: Throughout the book, when we use the phrases "web," "online," or "interactive" content, we're often not just talking about websites. The overarching goals and approaches of content strategy are relevant across every medium, platform, and device. As evolving technology continues to throw us one curve ball after the next, keeping a handle on our content—no matter where it is and who it's for—has become more critical than ever.

AND NOW, THE BOOK

Okay, that should be everything. Thanks for your patience with all of this preamble stuff.

You can go ahead and read the book now.

Enjoy.

REALITY

Behold, your content. Your business needs it. Your users want it. And yet no one seems quite sure what to *do* with it. A website redesign? A new CMS? Whatever the case, you're ready for a change. Let's put your content to work.

NOW

• •

YOU LIE AWAKE AT NIGHT thinking about your content. There's so much to fix. So much to plan for. You want to get ahead, but you can barely keep up with what's happening day-to-day. The last time you tried talking to someone about The Big Picture, the conversation was cut short by yet another "content emergency" that put you right back in reactive mode. And the content keeps coming. And coming. And coming.

Wow, one paragraph in and you're already crying a little?

Wipe away your tears, dear reader. Because, just for you, we've written a very short, non-scary chapter that introduces a few great ways to tackle even your toughest content challenges. (In fact, when you're finished, you'll think, "Gee, that wasn't so bad!" And that is our way of tricking you into reading the rest of the book.)

THINK BIG, START SMALL

Good news: you can significantly improve your organization's content in a fairly short amount of time by taking on any of the following efforts:

1. Do less, not more.

2. Figure out what you have and where it's coming from.

3. Learn how to listen.

4. Put someone in charge.

5. Take action … now.

Don't worry about having your proverbial ducks in a row before you dive in to content strategy. You don't need months of planning, a new staff, and a million dollars to do it. As Lao Tzu once said, "The journey of a thousand miles begins with one step." So let's get moving.

(Requisite "Lao Tzu quote in a book about strategy": check.)

#1: DO LESS, NOT MORE

Consultant David Hobbs once wrote, "Small websites are easier to manage than big ones. Since this is obvious, why don't more sites choose to be smaller?"

Of course, it's rarely an intentional choice. A website tends to take on a life of its own, its growth fueled by new products and services, changing brand campaigns, multiple publishers, constantly-shifting executive priorities, user-generated content, and more. Beyond the website, there are company blogs, Twitter feeds, press releases, email communications, and so on. The Great River of Content flows freely, rapidly flooding our customers with too much information and drowning its keepers (web editors and content managers) in the process.

Why do we need all this content? What's the point?

It seems that, in many organizations, more content is perceived as more selling opportunities, more user engagement, more help, more everything. But that's rarely the case. Generally speaking, content is more or less worthless unless it does one or both of the following:

- Supports a key business objective
- Fulfills your users' needs

If you assessed all of your current content, how much of it would meet these two simple requirements? Ninety-five percent? Seventy-five percent? Less than half? Are you chuckling ruefully and nodding your head yet?

Less content is easier to manage

When we talk about content getting published online, we often refer to it as going "live." Interestingly enough, we seem to think that our content will magically continue to maintain itself, without care and feeding. But spend 30 seconds tooling around almost any website, and you'll find this is patently untrue. Dead blogs. Outdated product descriptions. Broken links. Irrelevant search engine results.

The countless ways in which our web content dies on the vine are painful, and sometimes dangerous. It's one thing to change our brand voice on one media channel but ignore our web content. It's another to neglect content that may expose us to legal action by a customer or competitor.

By publishing less content, you will have less content to keep track of over time. It's a simple equation.

Less content is more user-friendly

Let's say you're ready to shop around for new auto insurance. You've written down a few top-of-mind insurance brands, including Geico and State Farm.

For starters, you open a browser and type in www.geico.com. You scroll down the home page just a bit, and here is what you see:

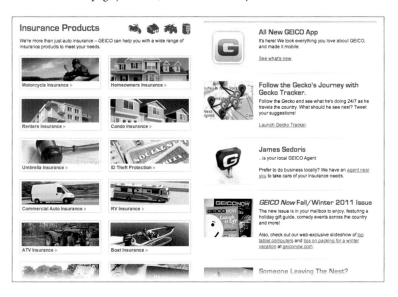

In the first three seconds of staring at this page, how confident do you feel that you'll find the information you're looking for?

Now you decide you'll give the Geico site search engine a try. You go to the search box and, type in *types of insurance.* Here are your results:

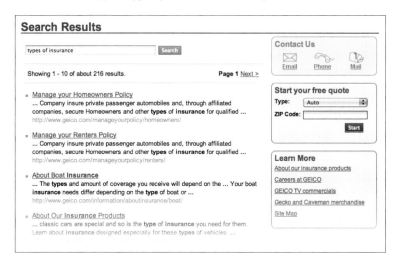

Hmm. Pretty worthless. How do you feel now? Frustrated? Resentful? Like leaving?

Too much content means information is harder to find, whether on the page or within your site. And that means it's harder for a customer to make a decision in favor of your product or service.

By contrast, take a look at State Farm's home page:

Clean. Concise. No-nonsense. You're in, you're out. And you're happy.

Less content costs less to create

How's that for a forehead-slapper?

By prioritizing useful and relevant over "wouldn't it be cool" and "just in case," you will magically dismiss at least half of your web content projects. That means you'll free up time and money for things like planning and measurement, two content-related tasks that often get short shrift in the race to do more online.

How can you begin to scale back on content? Ensure that your website content maps back to key business objectives and user goals. Create a web editorial calendar that specifies when and why new content will be published. And, moving forward, stop creating so much "just-in-case" content.

#2: FIGURE OUT WHAT YOU HAVE AND WHERE IT'S COMING FROM

You may dream of throwing out your old content and starting over. Reality would like to disagree with that idea. The content you have exists for one reason or another (even if they aren't good reasons), so before you can do anything with it, you're going to need to look at it. And the best way to accurately assess your current content woes is to conduct a content audit. An audit is an accounting of all currently published web content, with all the details recorded in a spreadsheet.

There are two basic kinds of audits—quantitative inventories and qualitative assessments. As information architecture expert Christina Wodtke says, an inventory catalogs "what's there" and an assessment answers the question: "is it any damn good?"* Depending on your situation you can do one or both.

Many people only think of audits when they are redesigning a website or migrating content to a new content management system (CMS), but audits are valuable at any time during the life of your content. In fact, **doing a content audit can be a terrific first step in building a business case for content strategy.** Simply putting everything together in one

---

*http://www.contentcompany.biz/articles/content_audit.html

big, scary-looking document and saying, "Yes, hello, have you seen what a disaster our website is lately?" can often spur people to action.

If you're dealing with a few hundred pages of content, you can and should take on a content audit immediately. If you're a larger organization with thousands of pages, a comprehensive content audit may simply be impossible to take on all at once. But that doesn't mean it shouldn't happen.

Ready to dig in immediately? Head on over to *Chapter 5, Audit.*

#3: LEARN HOW TO LISTEN

In our experience, most content problems exist simply because no one has ever asked the right kinds of questions about it: specifically, questions that focus on the people and processes that have an impact on its lifecycle. But even when organizations *are* asking the right questions, it's still only half of the equation. If you're going to get the right answers, you need to learn how to listen.

So who should you listen to? Your boss? The "experts"? That guy in the cube next to you who keeps reading over your shoulder and making comments about what you should do?

Generally speaking, we encourage you to…

- **Listen to your colleagues.** When it comes to content development and maintenance, people have specific needs and challenges that deserve to be acknowledged. Content ownership spans several roles and responsibilities: requesters, providers, creators, reviewers/approvers, and publishers. Their skills, tools, and perspectives must be assessed and considered as you develop your content strategy.

- **Listen to your users.** It's such an obvious statement, but it bears repeating (and repeating, and repeating): *No one knows better what your customer needs than your customer.* Although many of us truly believe we know exactly what our end users *really* want from us online, we can't know unless we ask them.

The best thing you can do is simply to stop assuming you already know the answers to the questions you've been asking. The harder you listen, the better you'll understand the rationale, politics, emotions, and motivations behind the reasons content-related decisions are (or aren't) being made. After all, you're not creating plans for some alternate reality in which everything perfectly unfolds according to The Strategy. You're planning for human beings and their ever-shifting needs and desires—also known as the real world.

For more information on how to craft the right questions for your content discovery process, see *Chapter 4, Alignment,* and *Chapter 6, Analysis.*

#4: PUT SOMEONE IN CHARGE

So. Who owns your web content?

Because we are psychic (we'll get to your love life and money issues later), we predict you will answer one of the following three ways:

- Lots of people.
- One person, except that person is mostly just in charge of fulfilling other people's content requests.
- Huh. I have no idea.

In other words … no one. No one owns the web content. That means no one has a real sense of what's out there: Is it up to date? Accurate? Still relevant? Most importantly, though, there's no one who actually gets to say "no." And that, dear reader, is bad.

Here's where we turn to the world of print publishing for some insight. Have newspapers been coming together day after day, year after year under distributed publishing models with no executive editorial oversight? No. Does a magazine make it to press thanks to a staff of writers whose marching orders are to acquiesce to every "emergency" content request? No. Also? No.

Your organization needs to have a person—or specific people—officially In Charge of All Things Web Content. This doesn't mean they need to be solely *responsible* for all web content creation, delivery, and governance. It means that they are charged with the same duties as an editor-in-chief (or executive editor) is for a print publication—overseeing high-level processes, budgets, and policies.

In a larger organization, it's likely that a team will work together to oversee content production and maintenance. The most important point, here, is that specific individuals or teams must be empowered to make content-related decisions ... especially when it comes to saying "no."

For more information on content workflow and ownership, see *Chapter 9, People*.

#5: TAKE ACTION ... NOW

Still feeling overwhelmed? That's okay. But we're going to ask you to take a deep breath and get ready to "fake it 'til you make it"—that is, to dive in and start swimming.

You have to start somewhere, sometime, so you might as well start now. There are lots of things you can do to get the ball rolling, whether or not you have approval or budget. For example, you can:

- **Ask your boss** which part of the website drives her craziest, then talk about how to approach improving it.

- **Start asking specific questions** about content—its purpose, the people who own it, and so on.

- **Educate yourself.** Read articles, participate in group forums, and listen to podcasts to better arm yourself with the right ammunition when your ideas come under fire.

- **Take colleagues to coffee or lunch**. Ask questions and listen carefully. Let them know you're on their side, even when they're at odds with each other. Start building trust by focusing people on the outcome: better content, less pain and suffering.

Most of all, don't be afraid to "fake it til you make it." You don't need to be an expert in content strategy to dive in and start getting things done.

YOU CAN DO IT!

Hey, check you out! Just a few pages in, and already you're acquainted with some of the tried-and-true methods of successful content strategists everywhere. Do you feel smarter? You look smarter. Go walk around and see if anyone notices.

Now comes the caveat. The reality is that, within most organizations, content has always been an afterthought—it's considered a byproduct of people's everyday efforts, rather than an asset that requires strategic consideration. No one accurately plans for it. No one has time to slow down and think about it. It's last on the list of things to spend time, money, or effort on.

You can handle this. You can make things right. But first, you need to understand what's wrong.

2 PROBLEM

GREAT CONTENT MEETS USERS' NEEDS and supports key business objectives. It engages and informs. It's well-written and intuitively organized. It keeps people coming back for more. But when content sucks—when it's overwritten, redundant, hard to find, irrelevant—people come, look, and leave. And, sometimes, they never come back. Most of the content we find online is simply in the way—even outdated or straight-up inaccurate. It's not doing what we need it to do. And somehow, we can't seem to get it fixed. It's always the elephant in the room, the one thing no one really wants to talk about. And man, that is one ugly elephant.

So whose fault is this content crisis, anyway? And who's going to clean up this mess?

NO FINGER-POINTING ALLOWED

It's very unlikely that your content challenges are caused by a single person or department. Content is a complex, hairy beast that depends on myriad people, technologies, and processes. When you can find a shared language to discuss your content challenges, you'll be better able to collaborate with your colleagues and identify solutions.

In this chapter, we'll look at some of the most common obstacles that keep us from turning bad content into better content:

- We treat content like a commodity.
- We don't have time to make a plan.

- We make deadly assumptions.
- Content is political.
- It's all too much, and we'll never move forward.

And now, let's take a few pages to bond together about our frustrations, hopes, and fears. You are not alone. It's time for content therapy.

How do you eat the elephant in the room?

WE TREAT CONTENT LIKE A COMMODITY

Delivering great content requires some kind of investment: user research, strategic planning, meaningful metadata, web writing skills, and editorial oversight. It requires real people and real resources to get it right, and it's not easy. That's why so many of our organizations are constantly looking for shortcuts to getting the content done. When we take that attitude, we start to see content as piles and piles of *stuff* that can be acquired at will. Here are some examples.

LET'S GO GET SOME CONTENT

To some, automatic aggregation of content (via RSS feeds or back-end algorithms) seems like a smart, painless alternative to the complicated, time-intensive, ongoing content creation process.

Similarly, the idea that we can pay to publish syndicated content under our own brand umbrella is wholly appealing. Sign on the dotted line, and fresh content will be delivered daily to your customers, courtesy of Custom Publisher Number Nine.

These aren't inherently bad ideas. In fact, working with content that's produced outside of your organization might be the right decision. But don't mistake these tactics as your answers to a long-term content strategy. Quality, relevant content can't be spotted by an algorithm. You can't just license it and then walk away. You need people to create or curate it.

LET'S PUBLISH AS MUCH CONTENT AS WE POSSIBLY CAN

There was once a client who was very interested in producing massive amounts of content on his website. His idea was that the more content he had:

- The better his search engine rankings would be
- The more value he would provide to his online audiences
- The more chance he had of creating "competitive differentiation" in his industry

Yes, content can do a lot. However, the website this client was hell-bent on creating would incur much greater costs than he could ever anticipate—in time, money, brand value, and customer satisfaction.

The more content you have, the harder it is to keep up with: it ages quickly, breaks our navigation systems, and starts piling up in ways we never expected. Suddenly, we find our users are struggling to complete the tasks they came to do—gather information, make a decision, get help, share relevant content with friends. A user doesn't want endless options. He wants the content he needs, when and where he needs it.

LET'S GET USERS TO GENERATE THE CONTENT FOR US

Although "user-generated content" may sound like "content you don't have to create," unfortunately there's a catch: You can't always depend on your audience to deliver the goods.

Let's say you own a technology company, and you're looking for ways to save money on phone-based customer support. Your website support section has been sorely neglected for years. You decide to launch a forum so that your customers can help solve each other's problems—a low-cost and, you believe, low-maintenance solution.

The forum launches. A few customers show up and pose questions. Other customers don't answer the questions, so your intern does. More questions trickle in. But with so few posts, and so few visitors, the forum feels like an empty restaurant, or a lame party that no one attended. Within a few months, the "last post" dates are looking old and tired. And your phone support costs haven't decreased by a cent.

What went wrong? Beyond the forum launch, there wasn't a plan. No one considered how to advertise or seed the forum, let alone drive user adoption.

If you're considering ways in which user-generated content can help you achieve business objectives and meet your end users' goals, be very realistic about the fact that it's hard work to make it work well. It *can* happen. But it's neither cheap nor automatic.

Speaking of cheap…

LET'S BUY CONTENT FOR $4

In 2009, Elizabeth Saloka wrote a Brain Traffic blog post titled, "Bangalore, We Have a Problem," that sums things up quite nicely:

> I've just stumbled on a company called Niche Writers India that offers web content for $4. Four. Dollars. That's, like, a sandwich. A gas station sandwich.
>
> Since when did web content become a cheap commodity? We're not talking about zipper togs and baby socks! We're talking about communication. Often, very technical and advanced communication.
>
> A sample of what you can expect for your four dollars:
>
> "Niche Writers India is the core when it comes to writing and this is what our clients feel about our content writing services

expanding to various domains and collaterals. We have bubbling, energetic and youthful warp and woof of writers!"

… Niche Writers India, though not in the manner it intends, makes a compelling case for the value of a good web writer. Hopefully after seeing this site, would-be value shoppers will decide to invest (more than $4) in their content.*

Of course, if you're comparison shopping based on price alone, you may think it's no big deal to sacrifice some degree of quality in order to save money. Don't do that. To truly differentiate yourself online, you must offer content that specifically and authentically embodies your brand. Your content must help your audience *do* something—better, smarter, and with greater ease.

Content that works for your business and that matters to your users is not a commodity. Done well, content can engage your users, answer their questions, and motivate them to take action. Done poorly, it will cause you to lose your audiences' attention and trust.

WE DON'T HAVE TIME TO MAKE A PLAN

Do any of these statements sound familiar?

"This needs to go on the home page."

"We should be on YouTube."

"I need this series of brochures converted for the web."

"We have to put our new mission statement in the About Us section."

"Let's write another dozen articles next month."

"We have to launch a blog."

Oh, really?

Why?

In your desire to deliver—to employers, clients, customers—you may tend to race right past strategy and into execution. It's not that you're not interested in doing the right thing. It's simply that you're under constant

*http://blog.braintraffic.com/2009/01/bangalore-we-have-a-problem/

pressure to deliver, to do *something* you can show your boss (and your boss's boss). You're expected to churn out requests, tasks, initiatives, and documentation as quickly as possible. That leaves very little time to step back, take a breath, and ask: "Why are we doing all this in the first place?"

Creating content might be a good tactic, but it isn't something you should do just because you *can*.

WE MAKE DEADLY ASSUMPTIONS

Let's say you're a subject matter expert at your company. There's a website redesign project happening, and you've agreed to take responsibility for your department's content. Hooray!

You know the project kicked off sometime last quarter, but you haven't heard much about it since then. Then one fine Tuesday around 2 p.m., an email pops up in your inbox…

> **SUBJECT: Website content: It's go time!**
>
> Hey, you! [Project manager] here. We're *finally* ready to have you start cracking on your share of the content. You should find all the information you need in the attachments:
>
> - Content inventory: Just look for your initials next to the pages you're supposed to write.
> - Page templates: You can build your documentation off of these.
> - Source material: This is what we could come up with. Hopefully it'll do.
> - SEO keyword guidelines: If you have any questions, just let me know.
>
> Okay! If we could see a first draft by A WEEK FROM TOMORROW (next Wednesday), that would be great. Just send it to me. Thank you!

From where you sit, this email might as well have been written in Sanskrit and sent from a land of unicorns and fairy dust. What is all this stuff? What's a page template? Why is your name next to random things in the "About Us" section?

This is exactly the kind of email you'll flag for review, then proceed to ignore for the rest of the week. Why? First, because it's confusing and overwhelming, and it makes you feel stupid. Second, you're fully booked through next week and the project manager is going to have to wait. And finally, you're just straight up resentful that the project manager would assume you could drop everything and do this.

Obviously, this situation sucks, as situations often do when our actions are based on assumptions and not reality. In this instance you (the subject matter expert) and the project manager made a tacit agreement at the beginning of the project: content shouldn't be too hard, because it's probably just some copywriting to support a bunch of content we already have. So let's talk about it later when we're closer to our deadlines.

Gong.

"DOING THE CONTENT" ISN'T LIKE COPYWRITING

When people think about the content development process, they often think about it sort of like baking a cake. Get the ingredients (gather source content); stir them up (compile, write, edit); cook it (finalize and approve); then frost it (add it to the design).

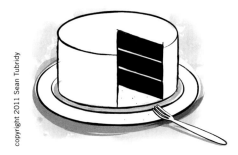

copyright 2011 Sean Tubridy

This is exactly the kind of thinking that leads to eleventh-hour content catastrophes. Because, in reality, "doing the content" is a whole lot more like running a bakery. There are countless details to consider. You have to manage people. Equipment is expensive, and it breaks. And what if the recipes are wrong or the donuts burn or you're losing money... you get the picture.

copyright 2011 Sean Tubridy

Getting your content right requires a whole lot more planning and upkeep than a print brochure. Helping others to understand this reality is a solid first step toward a successful content strategy.

CONTENT IS POLITICAL

Okay! After weeks of blood, sweat, and tears, you have a first draft of the content finished. Whew. Now, it's time to circulate it to the folks who need to review it.

Here's what happens next:

- The information architect hasn't seen this copy since it was "lorem ipsum" in the wireframes, and if she'd known it was going to say THAT, she would have taken a totally different approach.

- Marketing needs to sit down with you to ensure brand, messaging, and word usage are consistent with current campaign and style guidelines. (Which, didn't you hear? Those changed again three weeks ago. Here's the new 100-page manual.)

- The business owners, by the way, aren't too happy with the direction marketing is taking with this new campaign. They're totally missing the boat on at least 14 key benefits, here. Can you take a stab at incorporating those benefits into your copy?

- Legal is sick and tired of the way everyone seems to be willfully ignoring the fact that we are *required by law* to include this 800-word disclaimer on every page that mentions this one particular service. They would prefer to see it at the *top* of the page so that no one will miss it. While they're at it, they have some input about the way you've phrased a few hundred sentences.

- By the way, your CMS team is going to need two months to enter all this content into the CMS now, not two weeks. This is a lot more than they expected. Sorry.

Um. Hey. Whoa.

When it comes to web content, everyone has something to say. And when no one owns the content, priorities clash, and compromise can end up trumping best practices.

Making decisions that are primarily driven by many opinions puts you in danger of a free-for-all that seriously threatens your content quality, consistency, and effectiveness. As the adage goes, you can't make all the people happy all the time. Everyone has an agenda, but there's something you can agree on: You want your content to succeed, both for your business and for your users. A solid content strategy helps align stakeholders on priorities and desired outcomes, which makes life easier for everyone. For more, see *Chapter 4, Alignment.*

When it comes to content, no organizational unit stands alone. The table on page 24 shows how differing priorities and choices can impact content quality.

EVERY ORGANIZATIONAL UNIT HAS AN IMPACT

	IF THEY PRIORITIZE ...	AND NEGLECT TO CONSIDER ...	THE RISKS ARE ...
Business	Budget/ROI Schedule Deliverables	User experience Actual time to develop Project risks	Content doesn't meet user needs Missed deadlines delay project completion
Marketing	Talking about key features and benefits Search engine optimization Ability to measure response	Audience's priorities Customer-facing copy Maintenance post-launch	Content is more promotional than educational Writing suffers from "marketing speak" Content is launched then neglected
Advertising	Campaign-driven creative Highly interactive features Web 2.0 tools	Usability Existing content CMS restrictions or requirements	Content is more flash than substance Content is delivered in animation or graphics that can't be indexed or measured
User Experience	Audience needs and desires Research Visual design	Current state content analysis SEO considerations Planning for content	Business content objectives are overlooked or marginalized Desired content can't be completed by project launch date due to lack of source material, time, or budget
Information Technology	CMS or development requirements Production workflow	People involved in the content creation process Brand and messaging	Content may be published with a "fix-it-later" plan Final published content may not adhere to visual or editorial brand standards

IT'S ALL TOO MUCH AND WE'LL NEVER MOVE FORWARD

Figuring out what exactly is wrong with your world of content isn't always easy. But once you've identified and described the problems in detail, you have a whole new challenge on your hands: deciding what to do next. Of course, that's going to require several conversations with all kinds of people, and those people are going to have questions like:

- What *is* content strategy? How can it help me?
- When does content strategy start? How?

- Who does it? Where can we find these people? Who should they report to? Should we use outside firms to do the work?
- What are the roles and responsibilities people need to assume during the content strategy process?
- We have a website/mobile/CMS project looming (or already underway). Where exactly does content strategy fit in?

And, the question you'll hear the most will likely be the one that keeps you awake at night:

- Why should we invest in content strategy?

These are all excellent questions, and it's very reasonable to expect lots of discussion around them. Depending on your role on a project or in your company, that might be pretty intimidating. But here's what's great: When the time comes, you're going to be the expert everyone turns to for insight and information. You know why? Because you are going to keep reading this book. You are going to learn a whole lot about content strategy in not a whole lot of pages. And then you are going to put on your content strategy cape and get out there to save the content—to be the hero you were always meant to be.

Let's go! (Insert rousing orchestral music and confetti.)

3 SOLUTION

WHAT IS CONTENT STRATEGY? Is it a practice? A document? What does it include? Who's responsible for it? How is it implemented? Can we measure its success?

Your enthusiasm is palpable. We like it. We share it. Let's dig in.

RE-ENVISIONING CONTENT

Once we recognize content as a valuable business asset, we start to see it as more than just pixels or PDFs. And once we can identify goals for our content that serve both our organizations and our users, we can start to align our efforts to form a cohesive strategy. That strategy will then help us prioritize our content initiatives, streamline our efforts, and use our resources as effectively as possible.

In this chapter, we will:

- Explain what content strategy is (and is not).
- Examine the key elements of content strategy.
- Explore who does this work.

WHAT IS CONTENT STRATEGY?

Well, first of all, what is "content"? Content is what the user came to read, learn, see, or experience. From a business perspective, the content is the critical information the website, application, intranet, or any other delivery vehicle was created to contain or communicate.

Depending on who you are and what you need to do, content strategy can mean a few different things.

Content strategy:

- Defines how you're going to use content to meet your business (or project) goals and satisfy your users' needs
- Guides decisions about content throughout its lifecycle, from discovery to deletion
- Sets benchmarks against which to measure the success of your content

In summary: Content strategy guides your plans for the creation, delivery, and governance of content.

Sometimes, content strategy may focus specifically on the editorial, structural, or technical aspects of content. And sometimes, it may be an enterprise-wide effort that's directly tied to high-level business strategies. In either case, content strategy helps us find ways to better understand all aspects of our content, which means we can make smarter, more informed decisions about how we're going to select and execute our tactics.

WHAT ISN'T CONTENT STRATEGY?

When some people talk about their "content strategy," they're actually talking about *what* they plan to deliver online, and where. In this context, a content strategy may be described as:

- A series of educational articles
- A full-service, online knowledge base
- An employee blog post series
- A new tablet subscription service
- Social media accounts

These things, when combined, do not make up a strategy. They're just a bunch of tactics.

A strategy is an idea that sets the direction for the future. Once you've decided on your strategy, you can benchmark tactics against it simply by asking, "Will this help us get to where we're going?" Imagine your strategy as a lighthouse that keeps you headed in the right direction, no matter how stormy the waters may become.

HOW DOES CONTENT STRATEGY WORK?

As anyone practicing content strategy will tell you, the answer to this question is never cut and dried. In fact, it's what we're tackling in this book, which is sort of meta but let's move on.

Before we can talk about how content strategy works, we need to introduce what we refer to as "the quad"—an image that displays the critical components of content strategy. These are the things that affect whether or not your content ends up usable and valuable, both to your users and your business.

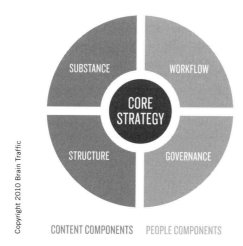

At the very center is the **core content strategy**. This defines how an organization (or project) will use content to achieve its objectives and meet its user needs.

The core strategy informs what the **content** will be and how it will be structured:

- **Substance:** What kinds of content do we need (topics, types, sources, etc.)? What messages does content need to communicate to our audience?
- **Structure:** How is content prioritized, organized, formatted, and displayed? (Structure can include IA, metadata, data modeling, linking strategies, etc.)

The core content strategy also informs how **people** (specifically content owners and overseers) will help drive the content lifecycle:

- **Workflow:** What processes, tools, and human resources are required for content initiatives to launch successfully and maintain ongoing quality?
- **Governance:** How are key decisions about content and content strategy made? How are changes initiated and communicated?

One breakthrough people often have when looking at the quad for the first time is realizing how important it is to address the people components as well as the content components. The relationship between substance and structure is fairly implicit: when you add content to a website, for example, the structure of that website might change. But what about how that new content will impact workflow? Does anyone need to review changes before they can go live? What happens if the content goes live and it's incorrect? Who's responsible for maintaining the new content? You get the point: **Content strategy connects real content to real people.** That connection is key to getting your content right.

WHO DOES CONTENT STRATEGY?

The easy answer is, "lots of people." And they do! Many people are practicing some type of content strategy in their current role … probably even you. But for now, let's look at the roles and responsibilities of a fully dedicated content strategist.

The content strategist is the person who is responsible for your content—for one project or your entire content landscape. This person:

- Is the advocate for the content throughout the team and organization
- Provides the background research and analysis that stakeholders need to make smart decisions about content
- Creates recommendations for the content based on business and user needs
- Works with the organization to implement the content online

Ideally, especially on large or complex projects, the content strategist solicits and synthesizes input from a variety of people, including web writers and editors, information architects, SEO practitioners, database managers, and subject matter experts. When needed, however, a good content strategist is often willing and able to embrace whatever role is necessary to deliver on the promise of useful, usable content.

WHAT EXACTLY DOES A CONTENT STRATEGIST DO?

What follows is a sample job description for a content strategist. Of course, depending on the structure and needs of your particular organization, roles and responsibilities will vary.

The content strategist is responsible for overseeing the success of content initiatives.

Collaborating closely with other key project stakeholders, the content strategist is critical to defining the content needs of websites and applications.

For each project, the content strategist will:

- Gather, audit, and analyze existing content relevant to project requirements.
- Collaborate with project leads to examine and analyze the content "ecosystem"—internal and external factors that impact the content—during the project discovery phase.
- Determine projects' overall content requirements and potential content sources.
- Ensure that the team aligns on content objectives, assumptions, risks, and success factors.

- Develop content strategy and plans based on client business objectives and user needs.
- Coordinate and collaborate with a team of experts in IA, SEO, social media, database management, metadata, and anyone else who is assigned ownership of an online initiative.
- Work with the web editor or web writer to oversee the development of all content to be included in the solution.
- Create taxonomies and metadata frameworks for grouping and tagging content.
- Develop content indexes and mapping documentation for the site.
- Understand and help implement content accessibility standards according to national law and organizational policy.
- Shepherd content through the creation process.
- Oversee content migrations and prepare documentation to do so.
- Work with database administrators to make necessary changes and updates.
- Ensure there is a plan for maintaining and governing content post-launch.

HOW IS CONTENT STRATEGY DIFFERENT FROM OTHER DISCIPLINES?

Well ... it might not be.

A content strategist's work isn't necessarily *separate or apart from* user experience, technical, or communications professionals. In fact, you might say the content strategist can work within, between, or inclusive of any of these disciplines, which may include:

Messaging and branding

Messaging and branding professionals specialize in defining what the "story" is behind the content. They answer questions such as: What are your brand values and attributes, and how will they inform the content? What do you want the user to learn or know or believe after reading your

CASE STUDY BECOMING A CONTENT STRATEGIST

In 2010, Shelly Wilson worked as the head of editorial in Northern Ireland's national education body's multimedia team, overseeing the content in the organization's print, web, and A/V materials. Deciding she was ready for a change, she applied for a position as a "content editor" at a web strategy and design studio called Front, located in Belfast. That's where she first encountered the concept of content strategy. With 15 years of experience in writing, editing, and marketing, both for print and for the Web, she thought it would be a fairly simple transition.

Though Shelly's skills and experience made her the perfect candidate for the job, she quickly realized there was a new skill she'd need to master as a content strategist: persuasion. Of course she had always persuaded authors to make changes, but she discovered that consultants use persuasion differently with clients. Many clients genuinely don't understand content, and that made it difficult for her to do her job. So rather than being a gatekeeper for quality and accuracy, she was now an ambassador, reaching out to clients and stakeholders to advocate for content. She learned how important it was to deconstruct, document, and articulate her rationale for each suggestion. She also began to invest a lot more time in showing rather than telling. She continues to hone her consulting skills to better deliver the strategic recommendations she was hired to create.

It's always tough to shift careers, and Shelly is still adjusting. "I'm not entirely comfortable yet, but I think you just have to get comfortable with being uncomfortable." And what's the upside? "Content strategy is more collaborative. The benefit is the additional perspectives. Working with so many people brings to light things you hadn't considered." And there's no greater thrill than getting all those people excited about good content.

content? Do we say different things to different users? Do we talk to the same user differently depending on his current task or length of relationship with the organization?

Web writing

Web writing is the practice of writing useful, usable content specifically intended for delivery online. This is a whole lot more than smart copywriting. An effective web writer must understand the basics of user experience (UX) design, be able to translate information architecture documentation, write effective metadata, and manage an ever-changing content inventory.

Information architecture

Information architecture involves the design of organization and navigation systems to help people find and manage information more successfully. An information architect who also focuses deeply on the content *substance* will define the content requirements for pages or content components of a website. This includes structural issues, messaging hierarchy, source content, maintenance requirements, and so forth.

Search engine optimization

Search engine optimization is the process of creating, editing, organizing, and delivering content (including metadata) to increase its potential relevance to specific keywords on web and site search engines.

Metadata strategy

Metadata strategy identifies the type and structure of metadata, also known as the "data about data" (or content). Smart, well-structured metadata helps publishers to identify, organize, use, and reuse content in ways that are meaningful to key audiences.

Content management strategy

Content management strategy defines the technologies needed to capture, store, deliver, and preserve an organization's content. Publishing infrastructures, content life cycles, and workflows are key considerations of this strategy.

CALL IT WHAT YOU WANT ... JUST GET IT DONE

It's utterly pointless to try and say, "This person isn't a *real* content strategist because she only does a subset of the activities that fall under the content strategy umbrella." Sure, there are content strategy generalists—professionals who can inform and perform the activities that affect every phase of the content lifecycle. But there are also professionals whose expertise runs deep in one specific area of content strategy, or whose work has direct impact on how a content strategy is created or executed.

Ultimately, the important thing is simply that someone is paying close attention to the critical questions that will make or break your content: why, what, where, for whom, by whom, when, how much, and what's next. It doesn't matter what you call it or who does it … as long as the work gets done!

SO, NOW WHAT?

Now comes the fun part.

The next six chapters will help you understand in depth how content strategy works. We'll talk about preparing for strategy, creating your strategy, and putting together your action plans for world domination through content. Which is totally possible.

Let's go!

DISCOVERY

Whether you know it or not, your current "world of content" extends far beyond what's on your website. It's made up of all the people, places and things that affect the way your content comes and goes. Let's go exploring…

4 ALIGNMENT

BECAUSE CONTENT TOUCHES just about every area of an organization, strategies only work when everyone is aligned and on the same page.

Alignment starts in the discovery process and continues, well, forever. At the beginning of the content strategy process, alignment is about providing your stakeholders with baseline information about the content, each other, and the strategy process. Then, for the rest of time, it means keeping people up to date, asking for input, and responding to questions. (Yes. Seriously. Forever.)

C'MON, PEOPLE NOW

Alignment isn't necessarily about creating consensus. It's about creating a common understanding. But how on earth are you supposed to accomplish that? In this chapter, you'll learn how to:

- Identify your stakeholders.
- Convince them to participate.
- Set the stage for alignment with a kickoff.
- Get them engaged.
- Keep them motivated throughout the project.

WHY IS ALIGNMENT SO IMPORTANT?

We've found that we can often predict how successful a content strategy will be within the first few weeks. How? We look at how receptive the project sponsors are to collaborating with others. It's our experience that people who are open to input and opinions succeed far more often than those who try to keep their projects under wraps.

Content strategy requires outreach and alignment. Why? Two reasons.

Lots of people affect your content

People throughout your organization are involved in content processes. The marketing and branding teams might be obvious players, but legal reviewers, subject matter experts, technologists, and many others have roles to play. Acknowledging and understanding their ideas, issues, and opinions will help you create a more informed, effective strategy.

Your content strategy affects lots of people

When you introduce a new content strategy, you're asking all of those people to change their habits, opinions, and accountabilities. That's a tall order. You'll need more than a fancy PowerPoint™ presentation to change people's behavior—you'll need their trust.

You'll need to help them understand the big picture. Ask for input and respond to questions. Show them where they can contribute and how they will benefit. The earlier you start, the better. So, hey, let's get started!

FIRST, IDENTIFY YOUR STAKEHOLDERS

When we talk about "stakeholders," we simply mean "people who matter to your project." Stakeholders can make or break your strategy project—so it's important to think carefully about who is necessary to the health of your content.

TYPES OF STAKEHOLDERS

When people think about picking stakeholders, they often try to get representatives from each of the departments in the organization. That's a good way to start. Having the right departmental representation is important.

However, as you create your list, you may want to think about functional categories, as well:

- **Strategic decision makers** are people who will be most impacted by your strategy and, therefore, deserve to have a significant amount of impact and input during the process.

- **Money people** are the folks that are funding your project. Maybe it's your boss, and your boss's boss. They are likely the ultimate decision makers on everything you do.

- **Champions** are people who will advocate for your project regardless of their relationship to the content. They see the value of content strategy and go out of their way to get others interested and invested.

- **Showstoppers** are individuals who have no "official" power, but could stop the project in its tracks (the CEO's henchman, for example). This category includes people who are politically necessary. You have to invite them, because they'll turn into showstoppers if they're not involved.

- **Interested others** are people who have tangential interests in your project. Maybe they have a very limited or indirect relationship to the content. Or, maybe they're considering a similar project of their own.

Considering these categories will make it easier for you to decide who needs to be involved, when, and in what capacity. Do they need to come to every meeting or just the big ones? Do you need to interview someone personally, or can you just send him a questionnaire?

Categories like this are certainly not a caste system. People can move from one to another, and sometimes be in two categories at once. **But, identifying your stakeholders by how they impact the project and not by their areas of expertise will help you understand how to involve them going forward.**

YOUR DAY-TO-DAY PLAYERS

The people in the "strategic decision maker" category often make up your core team. They come to all the meetings. They come up with the lion's share of ideas. And, they are the most important people to keep aligned. (The money people can be part of the core team, too, depending on their accessibility and interest.)

Of course, it's important to limit the core team to a reasonable size. What that size is depends on your situation. But, if you have a "core team" of 25 people, it'll be hard to get anything done. If you've got a big number of strategic decision makers, you'll have to decide who is most critical to have on the core team and who has the time to participate. Or, you can create several task forces that can work on different aspects of the project simultaneously.

Just be sure no one is excluded from the process altogether. Even the "interested others" should still be respectfully involved—whether you invite them to the biggest meetings or simply send them a quarterly email update.

NO ELITISM, PLEASE

It's tempting to just invite managers to represent their teams. But, in reality, the managers don't always know how things work in the content trenches. Be sure to include people who really know what's up, even if they're interns. A combination of people from all levels of the organizational hierarchy works best.

THEN, GET THEM INTERESTED

People are busy. They might not want to add anything else to their already triple-booked schedule. If you have key stakeholders you want to support or participate in your content initiatives, you may have to work at it.

You need to tell a compelling story (you're a content-savvy person, after all). Create a nice story arc, and present your case with the following elements:

- **The problem or opportunity:** What's going on with content—complete with some persuasive facts from the research or some particularly convincing examples on how content affects the stakeholder's bottom line or area of responsibility.

- **The urgency:** Why it's urgent to work on the content problem *right now.* (Competitive advantage? User needs? Business opportunity?)

- **The request for help:** Why you think they would be an asset to the team; what unique views they can provide. Make sure you tell them how much you respect their time, and outline your expectations for participation.

- **The players:** A description of who is participating (direct them to some of your project champions, if you've identified them already).

- **The payoff:** The benefits to them and the organization as a whole.

Most people like to be helpful and will agree to participate at some level. If someone important turns you down, respectfully ask them why. Resistance is often about lack of clarity, so you may be able to change their minds if you clear things up. If they still say "no," ask if they'd like occasional updates about content projects. Keeping them involved at any level is a win for you, if only a small one.

KICK OFF ON THE RIGHT FOOT

Usually, there is a formal kickoff meeting at the beginning of any content strategy project. This is where all the agreed-upon stakeholders come together for the first time. We often wait to host that bonanza until we have some research and analysis (see *Chapter 5, Audit,* and *Chapter 6, Analysis*) under our belts. That way, we can use early findings to put the project in context *and* ask the stakeholder group to fill in any analysis gaps. So, from the beginning, people are learning and contributing—getting the information exchange off to a good start.

As you're working toward early alignment, here's what should happen in the kickoff meeting.

EXPLAIN WHY YOU'RE THERE AND WHAT YOU'VE DONE SO FAR

If you want to get people on board, you need to be sure they feel included in the conversation. Using lots of industry lingo and failing to tell them what to expect will burn you every time. You'll need to:

- Explain what content strategy is
- Reiterate how content strategy will benefit the organization and the stakeholders

And, if you've already completed any audit or analysis work, you can discuss:

- What content exists today and what shape it's in (your audit findings)
- What the internal and external factors are that impact your content—highlighting user research, competitive research, and the content workflow process

HELP EVERYONE GET TO KNOW EACH OTHER AND THEIR ROLES

Probably the most important part of alignment in the discovery phase is to help stakeholders learn about each other. In large organizations, it's not uncommon for people to meet each other for the first time on a content project. Even in small companies, people may see each other in a new light. Helping people understand and engage with one another is a huge part of the job.

SET CLEAR EXPECTATIONS FOR WHAT COMES NEXT (AND FOR WHOM)

Lastly, you need to set the stage for the rest of the work. People will want to know:

- What is their role in the process?
- How much and how often will you need them to participate?
- What kinds of things will they be doing?
- Who are the decision makers and what is the decision making process?
- What are the immediate next steps?

The more they know, the more they'll feel some ownership in your content projects from day one. Remember, your stakeholders are your allies—or, if they're not initially, it's your job to find that common ground. You want them to trust you so they'll share the stuff that matters.

ENGAGEMENT DOESN'T STOP AFTER THE KICKOFF

At the beginning of a project, alignment is a major focus. But, it's important to make sure you keep the momentum going. How and when you solicit stakeholder input during the remainder of the project is unique to your situation. But no matter what happens:

- **Communicate and encourage participation:** Schedule regular meetings, host workshops, send regular updates, have Q&A sessions, etc. Be consistent as clockwork—it's another way to inspire trust.

- **Listen and respond:** Always take the stakeholders seriously. Respond to their ideas and insights in a respectful, timely way.

- **Distribute documentation:** Make sure people always have documentation in hand—so they can follow along in meetings and have reference materials whenever they want to refresh their memories.

- **Celebrate milestones:** Highlight milestones and other progress. Be sure everyone knows how he or she contributed in positive ways.

- **Set expectations:** Make sure people always know where they stand. What is their role in the project? What do they have to do next?

Alignment is a never-ending, but highly rewarding, process. Just think of the smart people in your stakeholder group. When you harness all that brainpower, you're bound to meet—and exceed—your business and user goals.

GO, TEAM, GO

Alignment is a huge first step as you head into your discovery phase. Once you've rallied the players, you're ready to tackle your content together.

In the next two chapters, we'll dig deep into your content (audits) and examine the world in which it lives (analysis).

Are we aligned on this plan? Terrific. Onward.

5 AUDIT

SOMETIMES, WE'LL ASK a conference audience, "How many of you know exactly what you have on your website, where it lives, and who owns it?"

Inevitably, even in rooms of several hundred people, only one or two people raise their hands.

This, friends, is a problem. To make even the most basic decisions about your content—like deciding where to focus your resources and budget—it's good to know how much content you have, where it lives, what it's about, and whether it's any good.

And to know these things, you need to do a content audit.

SEEING IS BELIEVING

A web content audit is an accounting of the content your organization currently has online. More often than not, when you're finished (or even midstream), the results are unbelievably valuable. As we said in the first chapter, an audit can be one of your most powerful tools when making a business case for any web content project.

When you finish this chapter, you'll understand:

- Why audits are important
- What kinds of audits are most common
- How to record your audit findings
- How much content you need to evaluate
- How to share your results

Let's get to it.

THINKING ABOUT SKIPPING THIS CHAPTER? DON'T.

"We know the basic gist of what's on our site." "Somebody else in our organization must have done this before." "I hate spreadsheets and don't want to waste my valuable time on this."

Here's the deal. No matter how unnecessary or unpleasant an audit may look to you, don't skip it. This process isn't just about building up a nice spreadsheet of URLs and page titles. Audits can:

- Help you scope and budget for a content project
- Give you a clear understanding of what you have and where it lives, even if only to begin thinking about maintenance or content removal
- Serve as a reference for source (or existing) content during content development, making it a highly efficient tool for writers and other content creators to keep track of what they have to work with

CAN'T ROBOTS DO THIS FOR ME?

At this point you may be thinking, "An audit sounds awfully time-consuming. Surely there are widgets that can audit my website automagically!"

The answer is yes—there are "audit tools" that can crawl sites and capture basic information, such as titles and links. Some CMSes have audit-like features, too. During the audit process, this kind of technology can be extremely helpful and, in some cases, necessary. **But beware.** Technology doesn't replace the context provided by human review. If you really want an in-depth understanding of your content—substance, quality, accuracy—people power is the best way to go.

CASE STUDY THE VALUE OF AN AUDIT—SAVING TIME, SAVING MONEY

Carrie Hane Dennison works for a full-service web development firm called Balance Interactive in Springfield, Virginia. She says that her clients are starting to realize they need content strategy, even if they don't know what it is.

Although clients aren't always looking for a line item called "strategy," Carrie finds ways to address content strategy. She prefers to do so early in a site redesign, but sometimes works with clients after content requirements are already in place. At either stage, using an inventory is one way Carrie helps her clients understand and address strategy. She explains to clients that, for every 5 hours they spend auditing near to the beginning of a project, they might save 20 hours at a later stage, preventing project delays.

After conducting an inventory of existing and needed content, Carrie asks her clients to spend time thinking about messaging, or considering the number of hours needed to complete the writing or content migration. She recalls one client who took one look at the inventory and said, "There's no way I can get this all done." Rather than setting up her own staff to fail, the client hired Carrie's team to help migrate the content. The result was an on-time launch of the new website, rather than a month late.

That's really the point of an audit: You can anticipate problems before they arise, and avoid derailing your project. All of that time and money may seem daunting at the beginning, but Carrie's clients are impressed when the investment means they're able to launch a better site, on schedule.

Technology *can* help you get:

- **Quick wins:** When you have a very limited timeframe to build a business case or to prepare for an upcoming web project, technology can help. For example, if you want to understand the total volume of content on a website, an audit tool can give you a ballpark estimate in a hurry.

- **A head start:** Auto-audit tools can save you tons of time by creating a complete list of all of your content, as well as some basic info about each content piece. Additionally, in sites without traditional navigation, CMS-driven tools may be the only way to get a complete list without going totally insane.

- **Neutral data:** In organizations large and small, content discussions can get political. In this case, technologically generated, raw, undisputed data about your content can be your best friend.

Even with all of the technical shortcuts available, many content strategists prefer to do audits by hand. There is simply no better way to fully comprehend all of your existing content.

COMMON TYPES OF AUDITS: CHOOSE YOUR OWN ADVENTURE

Here's the single, most important thing you need to know about audits: **The kind of audit you do depends on what you want to learn.** There is no one perfect format, size, or timing for an audit; there are many different (and totally valid) ways to audit your content. What you pick depends on your goals.

Here are a few of the most common content audits.

AUDIT TYPE	DESCRIPTION	WHY	WHEN
Quantitative inventory	A list of all the content you have—just like the inventory of the products in a warehouse or store	Demonstrate magnitude and complexity of your existing content	Before content strategy work begins (right now)
Qualitative audit: Best practices assessment	A comparison of your content against industry best practices, usually done by a third-party, unbiased assessor	Prioritize content efforts (usually by identifying the lowest quality content and gaping holes)	Before strategy begins or in the early stages of strategy development
Qualitative audit: Strategic assessment	An invaluable, in-depth look at how your content measures up to your strategic goals (business or user)	Identify gaps between where you are and where you want to go; get insight into what resources you'll need to get there	Works best after your core strategy and key strategic recommendations are complete

WHICH AUDIT IS RIGHT FOR YOU?

There's no hard and fast rule, here. You can choose to do one of these audits, all three, or create your own audit format. No matter what you choose, doing a thorough audit will give you priceless information about your content.

Start by setting clear goals for your audit. These will help you determine which audit(s) you choose and what information they capture. Think about:

- What you want to learn (and why)
- What you need to prove (and to whom)
- How long you have to get the audit done (be realistic)
- Where you are in the content strategy process (if you're not sure, see the next five chapters ...)

Let's take a closer look at each of the audit types.

QUANTITATIVE INVENTORY: JUST THE FACTS

The goal of a quantitative inventory is to learn what you have, where it lives, and a few other basic stats. No frills. Just objective facts.

A quantitative inventory is the quickest and easiest way to get some insight into your content at the beginning of a project. BUT. By simply cataloging the number of pages, downloadable PDFs, dynamic content modules, video clips, and other "live" web content for which your organization is responsible, you can wake up stakeholders to the magnitude of your content—and the budget you need to create/maintain/fix it. Cha-ching.

What to record

Here's a list of the most common bits of data recorded in quantitative inventories. Title/Topics is a must-have. The other factors you choose depend on—you guessed it—your audit goals:

- **ID:** Assign an identification number or code to each piece of content. (See page 57 for more information.)
- **Title/Topics:** For a web page, this is likely the title of the page. For a content module, you may choose to use the heading or subhead. If there is no title of the content piece or page, include a short description of the key topics or themes covered.
- **URL:** Record only where applicable.
- **Format:** Make a note of the technical format of the content, such as text, video, PDF, etc.

- **Source:** Specify whether the content is created in-house, by a content partner (newsfeeds, articles, blog posts, and so on), or by your users. *Note:* For content created by your internal team, if you can, note who creates, approves, and publishes each piece of content. This information can be enormously helpful when you begin to ask questions about why certain content was done a certain way, or when you want to confirm it's okay to change or remove the content. We'll examine this topic in detail in *Chapter 9, People.*

- **Technical home:** If you're dealing with a very large site that's hosted on a number of different servers or platforms, take note of where the content lives within your technical infrastructure. For example, is the content in a content management system (CMS), inventory system, or fed to the site via an API? Sometimes content may be stored in very strange places, so be prepared to do some digging.

- **Metadata:** Metadata is "data about data." In this case, we're talking about attributes (such as keywords and tags) assigned to each piece of content. These valuable data nuggets help people find content on search engines, on your site, and in your CMS. When planning findable, functional content during the strategy phase, you'll need to know what metadata exists. If you don't know where to find your metadata, your friendly IT colleague, web developer, or SEO consultant should be able to help.

- **Traffic/usage statistics:** There are analytics available for almost any kind of online content. If it's feasible, get the skinny on how people are using (or not using) each piece of content. An internal analytics person or a representative from your analytics provider can often help you get the information you need.

- **Last update:** When was the last time somebody in your organization paid attention to this piece of content? Most CMS systems record a "last update" date—and that information can give you hints about the significance of the content, the content workflow, and more. Just don't make any drastic assumptions—keep it in context.

- **Language:** If you have content in multiple languages, you'll want to record the language or dialect used on each piece of content.

Note: robots welcome here

While it's always helpful to review your content personally, quantitative inventories are where the robots really shine. Because quantitative inventories are about collecting raw data (no human judgment required), the right technical tools can save you time and energy.

QUALITATIVE ASSESSMENTS: DEEPER DIVES

Seeing what content you have and where it lives is helpful, but only to a point.

Many a site map has been constructed based solely on page titles. But when it comes to qualifying the usefulness of content, a page title doesn't tell you what the content actually says, or if it's useful to your audience. That's where a qualitative audit comes in.

A qualitative audit analyzes the *quality* and *effectiveness* of the content.

The key distinction between quantitative inventories and qualitative audits is human judgment. Qualitative audits are a robot-free zone. An actual human being has to look at each piece of content and evaluate it based on defined characteristics.

In our chart on page 50, we listed two kinds of qualitative audits. Both take the quantitative inventory and go a few steps further:

- **Best practices assessment:** Usually done early in the project, a best practices assessment looks at your content from an outsider's point of view. It measures your content against best practices and user needs. It helps you understand if your content is useful, usable, enjoyable, and persuasive to your audience—or what you need to do to make it so.

- **Strategic assessment:** A strategic assessment is the most full-featured of all audits. Once you have a strategy in place, a strategic assessment gives you an idea of how your existing content aligns with it. Where are the gaps? What needs to change? What's terrific as it is? A strategic assessment can combine factors from a best practices assessment with strategy-specific criteria. Note that this is often informed by analysis and recommendations—we talk about a lot of this in the next chapter.

Sample qualitative audit factors

In addition to the information gathered in a quantitative audit, there are dozens (if not hundreds) of possible subjective factors you can review during a qualitative audit. We generally choose 5–6 factors based on the situation. The table on page 55 shows a few of our favorites.

Create your own factors

As we mentioned, the table only includes a few sample audit factors. Feel free to be creative and think of your own. Just be sure you can:

- Evaluate the factor by looking at individual pieces of content (not groups or categories of content)

- Use the factor to assess most or all of the content (i.e., not just one type of content)

- Develop clear, specific guidelines for measurement (including ratings or categories)

THE MORE (AUDITORS) THE MERRIER

If you're auditing 1,500 pieces of content, one person can handle it. (Yes, really!) But if you're looking at 10,000 pieces, you're going to want some help.

When you share audit responsibilities, it's absolutely imperative that your audit criteria, ratings, etc., are crystal clear. In addition to defining and communicating the criteria, you may want to:

- Have one person test the audit criteria before splitting up the work

- Create some examples of each criterion or rating

- Have regular check-ins with the audit team and spot-check each other's work

- Make sure that in addition to ratings and pre-defined lists, auditors have a notes field to jot down anything out of the ordinary or explain their thinking

When it's all over, you can commiserate about the agony of audit eyeball (where you can no longer look at the screen without seeing double).

QUALITATIVE AUDIT FACTORS

FACTOR	DESCRIPTION	SCALE OR CATEGORIZATION
For use in either best practices or strategic assessments		
Usability	When it comes to online content, usability is key. Does your content have short or long paragraphs? Subheads? Do you think there are too many text links? Too few? Are there typos or poor quality graphics? Assess each piece of content.	Use a rating scale (e.g., 1–5; poor-satisfactory-excellent; etc.)
Knowledge level	If your subject matter is scientific or otherwise complex, you may want to judge how much prior knowledge your user needs to understand your content. It's okay to have Ph.D.-level content and content for beginners, but you need to know which is which.	Use a rating scale
Findability	Content is neither useful nor usable if no one can find it. Does the content appear in the navigation or easily on site search? Is the metadata appropriate?	Use a rating scale
Actionability	After users finish the content, you want to be sure they know what to do next. Decide how clear the call to action is—whether you want them to push the proverbial "buy button" or simply tell a friend about your content.	Use a rating scale
Audience	Not every page of your site is for every user. If you have several main audiences for content, define the top 3–5 in advance. For each piece of content, choose the primary and secondary audiences from a pre-defined list. Also, remember, your audience prioritization may change after your strategy is complete.	Pick from a pre-defined list of target audiences
Accuracy	Inaccurate or out-of-date content can mislead your users, be plain embarrassing, or, at worst, expose you to a lawsuit. You may need to engage subject matter experts in this part of the audit to help identify what's outdated or just flat out wrong.	Use a rating scale
For use in strategic assessments only		
Business value	Along with satisfying your audience, content has to benefit your business to make it worth your time and energy. So, decide if each piece of content helps achieve a business goal or KPI. If so, which one?	Pick from a pre-defined list of goals or KPIs
Message	During your strategy development, you'll likely define key messages you want the content to communicate to your audiences. Which, if any, of the key messages does each piece of content support?	Pick from a pre-defined list of key messages
Brand/voice appropriateness	Does your content accurately reflect your organization's brand? Evaluate your content on whether it lives up to your brand promise, style guidelines, or company culture.	Use a rating scale

AUDIT SPREADSHEETS: CHOOSE YOUR WEAPON

Back in the old days (like, 2005), auditing was so easy. Web content = website pages. The format of audit findings was always the same: a simple list of pages, ordered by navigation, in a spreadsheet.

Today, getting a handle on your content can be more complex. Content isn't necessarily assigned to a single page on a website anymore—in fact, it might not be on a website at all. Even if it is, it might be displayed differently depending on the user's behavior, preferences, or device (computer, phone, tablet, etc.).

Spreadsheets are still the go-to format for most audits, but the tools are evolving to accommodate new kinds of content. Let's take a look at a few of the more popular options and how they work.

THE BASIC SPREADSHEET: OLD FAITHFUL

If you have a traditional website—where content is assigned to a specific page within a fixed navigation scheme (usually a home page with lots of neatly organized pages underneath)—a basic spreadsheet is the tool for you. Here's an example of a basic spreadsheet for a fake plant nursery website:

Pretend Nurseries, Inc. Website

Page ID	Page title	URL
0.0	**Home page**	http://pretendn
1.0	About us	http://pretendn
1.1	History	http://pretendn
1.2	Leadership team	http://pretendn
1.2.1	Bill Springdale, founder	http://pretendn
1.2.2	Judith Monroe, president	http://pretendn
1.3	Customer service policy	http://pretendn
2.0	**Products**	http://pretendn
2.1	Perennial flowers	http://pretendn
2.1.1	Aster plants	http://pretendn
2.1.1.1	Snowdrift aster	http://pretendn
2.1.1.2	Springdale signature aster	http://pretendn
2.1.1.3	Apollo dwarf aster	http://pretendn

To audit your site, you simply click through every page of your site (usually in order) and record the information in an outline format. List major website sections as your top-level "parent" (or primary) sections. Then plug in pages and modules as "children" (or secondary, tertiary, and so on) sections or pages in each main section. Most of the time, the pages are numbered the same way you'd organize a document outline (1.0, 1.1, 1.1.1, and so on).

A note about ID numbers

If you don't already have a numbering system for your web content, it's a good idea to start one during the audit process. By assigning a unique ID to each page or component, you have an easy way to reference each piece of content, categorize content for analysis, and get an understanding of how pieces of content relate to each other. Lastly, a number system will help you link your audit findings to other web project documentation—the number of a specific piece of content can correspond to the content strategy recommendations for that content, etc.

SPREADSHEET 2.0: WHEN CONTENT FLEXES AND CHANGES

As we mentioned above, today's smarty-pants programmers have made it possible to customize website content based on who you are, your past behavior, or the device you're using. (For example, people viewing a page on a mobile phone may only see half of the content available on a computer.)

When your site has these bells and whistles, variations need to be included in your audit. If your site has a set structure (where the navigation is basically the same for everybody), you're in luck. You can still do the inventory in an outline manner with some small adjustments. Start by choosing one version of the content to be the root of your inventory (the primary user group, the most common device, etc.) Then amend your ID system and spreadsheet to indicate variations.

Back to our nursery example. Let's say the nursery website has two audiences: the general public and professional landscapers. People who are logged in as professionals get expanded or different information. In this (very simple) example, we've added ":g" to the end of the ID numbers of pages targeted to the general public, and ":p" for versions of the pages for professionals.

2.0:g	Products
2.0:p	**Products**
2.1g	Perennial flowers
2.1:p	Perennial flowers
2.1.1:g	Aster plants
2.1.1:p	Aster plants
2.1.1.1	Snowdrift aster

In these types of audits, consistency is key. Regardless of the numbering system you select, make sure it's used correctly throughout the audit.

INDEXED INVENTORY: WHEN THINGS GET REALLY HAIRY

Now come the sites, apps, and content channels that are so incredibly flexible it seems like there is no navigation at all. Or, there really isn't any navigation. Just tags. Or facets. Or something.

Whatever the situation, the content in question cannot be audited in an outline format. You can still use a spreadsheet for your audits, but you likely need to:

- Get a list of content pieces from the backend. It's really hard to get a complete list of content pieces by clicking around. So, if you're unfamiliar with the backend system, it's time to make friends with an IT or CMS-focused colleague.

- Document (or find the documented) user characteristics or behaviors that cause the system to display each piece of content. Again, the backend people probably have this all worked out on a fancy model somewhere.

- Categorize the content into groups for analysis such as topic, product type, audience segment, or internal content owner. Create a meaningful numbering/indexing system based on your categorization. (If the CMS does this for you, too, hooray! But, often the CMS numbering system is too abstract for the purposes of an audit analysis. Boo.)

Our nursery audit might look like this:

Pretend Nurseries, Inc. Website

Content ID	Topic
Products	
Prod.Per	**Perennial flowers**
Prod.Per.1	Aster (general)
Prod.Per.2	Snowdrift aster
Prod.Per.3	Springdale signature aster
Prod.Per.4	Apollo dwarf aster
Prod.Per.5	Daisy
Prod.Per.6	Daylilly
Prod.Bul	**Bulbs**
Prod.Bul.1	Crocus
Prod.Bul.2	Daffodil
Prod.Bul.3	Hyacinth
Prod.Shu	**Shrubs & Hedges**
Prod.Shu.1	Evergreen shrubs

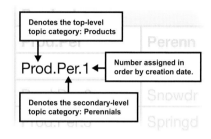

Now this is a simple example; things often get significantly more complicated. Indexing systems get tricky, and, in some cases, it's easier to create an audit database instead of a spreadsheet. Make the choice based on your audit goals, the people working on the audit, and the size of the mess you might be in.

DO YOU REALLY NEED TO LOOK AT ALL OF THE CONTENT?

It depends. If you have less than 5,000 pages/pieces of content, you should probably look at all of it. Yep. All of it. Why? Because you can: it's humanly possible to do so.

But what happens if you have 25,000, 100,000, or 100,000,000 pieces of content? Or, you don't have enough time to review 5,000 pages? When looking at every page is not an option, you have two choices: content sampling or rolling audits.

CONTENT SAMPLING

One way to audit huge piles of content is to review a "representative sample" of your content.

Choosing your sample

The challenge with creating a sample is deciding what content should be included. Sure, you could just do a randomly generated selection of content items, but usually it's better to make your sample more intentional by basing it on what you want to learn.

Brain Traffic's Christine Anameier suggests considering the following criteria when selecting your audit:

- **Content objectives:** If 70% of the site content is designed to increase sales and 25% is dedicated to customer support, your sample set can reflect those percentages. The remaining 5% (such as job postings or corporate philanthropy information) can be sampled lightly or not at all.

- **User groups:** Divide sample content by user group—ensuring content for each of your major user segments is represented. Better yet, prioritize the user groups and sample more pages for the highest priority users.

- **Traffic:** Site analytics can show you which pages or sections get the most visits and which get the least. Depending on your business goals, you may choose to focus on the high-traffic content, low-traffic content, or a combination of all traffic levels.

- **Content ownership:** It may not be possible to include work from all teams of content contributors, but it's helpful to get a good mix from people that regularly create your content. If the sample consists mostly of one group's work, it may not reflect the content as a whole and other teams may not embrace the audit findings.

- **Update or maintenance frequency:** Some content is maintained lovingly. Other content is left to go stale. If either of these two scenarios is over-represented in your sample, the results of the audit will be skewed—creating a false sense of pride or doom.

- **Depth:** It's tempting to audit only top-level pages of a website, but with today's search tools, customers may never even see your top-level pages. The "deeper" content is often where your customers run into major problems. In his book, *Killer Web Content*, Gerry McGovern writes, "I come across many websites where there is a well-designed top level with quality content. However, when you click down a few levels, everything changes—it's like walking out of a plush hotel straight into a rubbish dump." So you may want to look at a cross-section from all content levels.

When choosing your sample, how much content is enough?

There's no rule or benchmark for picking the perfect sample size. It would seem like the more content you could review, the better off you'd be. That's somewhat true, but mostly you just have to **look at enough content to see patterns emerge, answer your questions, or reduce uncertainty**.

On a relatively small site (i.e., 10,000 pieces of content), you might need to look at half of the content before the patterns become obvious. For a million-page site, you might decide to look at only 1% of the content. That's still 10,000 pages ... so you're not exactly off the hook. But, you should begin to recognize some kind of valuable patterns. You won't have the same level of certainty about your findings as you did with the smaller site audit, but you'll have some ideas. And you probably aren't going to learn anything else by auditing another 1,000 or 10,000 items—comparatively, the percentage of items reviewed is still so low that the change in the margin of error is microscopic.

Here's a rough table of suggested sample sizes (based on common market research sampling practices):

TOTAL NUMBER OF PAGES/PIECES	SAMPLE SIZE
<5,000	Varies
10,000	5,000
25,000	7,000
50,000	8,000
100,000	9,000
>1,000,000	10,000–16,000

If you can't make these benchmarks or just want to ignore them, don't sweat it. Adjust the sample size to your resources and time. Just about any sample will tell you something as long as you (and the people you show your results to) understand what content you reviewed and why.

ROLLING AUDITS

Another effective way to audit large sites is a rolling audit—an audit that basically never ends. Lou Rosenfeld (Rosenfeld Media) says an audit or inventory "shouldn't be something that you allocate the first two weeks of your redesign to; allocate 10 or 15 percent of your job to it instead."

It works like this: In January, you audit one area of a website. In February, you audit a different area. In March, you move onto a third, and so on. Eventually, when all of the content of the site is audited, you start over with the first category again. (It doesn't have to be monthly, either.)

The benefit of a rolling audit is that more content gets looked at, in a more careful manner, more often. This works best when stakeholders can agree to focus the first phases of the audit—and the content strategy—on a few discrete areas of the site.

And, guess what? On a super huge site, you can do a rolling sample of each area of the site instead of a rolling audit. It's like a dream come true, really.

TABULATE YOUR RESULTS

When you've finished evaluating all of your content, stop and celebrate. Just bask in the glory of that completed spreadsheet. Have a cupcake! Take a nap!

Okay, that was fun. Back to work.

By this time, the audit team likely has a good idea of where your content shines and flounders. But, there's nothing like cold, hard numbers to drive home the point. So, take the time to tabulate the results and look for patterns. You'll be able to answer questions like:

- How much content do we have, exactly? Do we have more in some categories than we would have expected?

- Which areas of content score especially high or especially low on any specific factor?

- Do we have a disproportionate amount of content for one audience segment?

- How much of our content is out of date or inaccurate?

When you crunch the numbers, you often find some pretty insightful stuff.

SHARE YOUR FINDINGS

At this point, you may be totally enamored with your spreadsheet and raw data—we are, too—but chances are your business stakeholders won't share your devotion.

For them, you'll need an **audit report**. Prepare the report in whatever format suits your audience: it can be a presentation or a full-scale document. You just need to convey the results of the audit and provide a reference for future discussions.

An audit report usually has three parts: an overview of the audit process, a path to access the raw data, and the findings report.

OVERVIEW OF THE PROCESS

First, your report should provide a brief description of the audit process. This will help make your findings more understandable and believable. You might want to include:

- **Goals of the audit:** Why you did the audit, what you hoped to learn, and what you want to do with the results.

- **Audit factors and measurement criteria:** A brief overview of what was measured and how.

- **Scope:** What areas of content were audited and why. If the content is particularly time-sensitive, you may need to include a date range as well.

PATH TO RAW DATA

Some people who see your audit report are going to want to see the data. If you so choose, you can provide them with a link to the spreadsheet. But, don't just let them loose with it. Provide a spreadsheet guide that explains how the spreadsheet works and alleviates any confusion.

FINDINGS REPORT

Third, and most importantly, you'll want to provide your audit findings. Your findings can include:

- A summary of overall conclusions and recommendations
- A description of each audit factor
- Data summaries per factor
- Factor-based themes or suggestions (with examples, when possible)

The report you create depends on the people who will see it. How much do they need to know? How much do they want to know? You may have different reports for different groups of people for the same audit. Here are some examples of what you might see in an audit report.

Formal detailed report

In this example, the auditor pulls out all the stops. This is a formal report made for an audience that craves details. In this example, the audit examined types of content formats used throughout the site. On this page of the report, you have:

1. A description of the audit factor
2. Graphic depiction of the results
3. Data cross-referencing site section and format
4. Key findings and analysis about the factor

1

2

CONTENT FORMAT (REFERENCE SECTION)

Is the content mostly text or a different medium, and (if text) how long is it?

For the reference section of the site, we have decided that articles between 3-10 paragraphs are ideal (other areas of the site differ). For text content, we took a rough paragraph (P) count based on medium-length paragraphs. Short paragraphs and bullet points were counted as partial paragraphs. All counts were approximate.

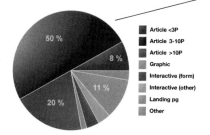

50 %

8 %

11 %

20 %

- Article <3P
- Article 3-10P
- Article >10P
- Graphic
- Interactive (form)
- Interactive (other)
- Landing pg
- Other

3

Value	Meaning	TOTAL	Home	Per.	Bulb	Vine	Shrub	Grass	Tree	Rose	Fert.	Supplies
Article <3P	Article-style text (<3 paragraphs)	8%	0%	0%	5%	3%	11%	21%	14%	6%	13%	12%
Article 3-10P	Article-style text (3-10 paragraphs)	50%	46%	47%	59%	71%	49%	53%	42%	44%	49%	38%
Article >10P	Article-style text (>10 paragraphs)	20%	9%	30%	15%	15%	24%	17%	27%	29%	23%	10%
Graphic	Chart or graphic with caption, little or no article-style text	1%	4%	3%	0%	0%	0%	0%	0%	3%	0%	5%
Interactive (form)	Action form, survey, etc.	3%	12%	5%	1%	2%	1%	0%	1%	4%	0%	9%
Interactive (other)	Content that users explore through clicking	3%	0%	1%	8%	1%	1%	0%	0%	1%	0%	6%
Landing pg	Content is only, or primarily, links (primary purpose is navigation)	11%	25%	11%	9%	9%	11%	9%	11%	8%	15%	18%
Other	Content not fitting above types	2%	1%	3%	2%	0%	2%	0%	5%	3%	0%	4%

KEY FINDINGS

Content length

4

Pages **under three paragraphs** (**8%** of the section) often have too little content to be effective as a standalone page. In many cases, these were very brief introductions to a long PDF-format report. Where the report is not aimed at a general audience, or where your site analytics show that few users click on the report link, it's especially important that these report introductions be expanded so that they cover the important points as standalone pieces. The topics with the highest proportion of short content were Grasses and Trees.

With our subject matter, pages **over ten paragraphs** (**20%** of the section) may risk losing readers partway through. In most topic areas, about 15% of their content is more than 10 paragraphs; the topics with the highest percentages of long content were Shrubs (24%), Trees (27%), and Roses (29%). (Also Fertilizers at 23%, but we've decided that this part of the site is a lower priority.)

(Findings continued on the next page)

Casual summary report

This report is more casual—possibly directed at a core team who is familiar with the audit and the content. It doesn't go into the details, but gets the high-level messages across. This page includes:

1. Summary of the key finding for this factor

2. A bit of detail that clarifies problem areas

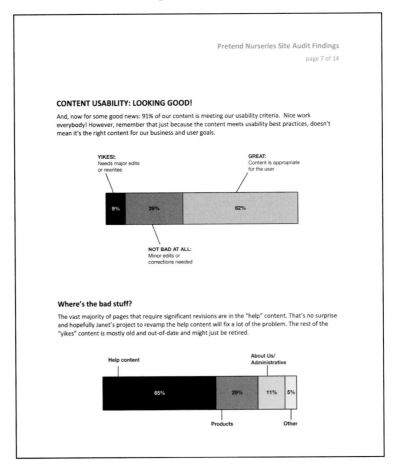

Presentation-style report

This slide is from a presentation that might summarize a report or may be the report itself. The slide headline summarizes the key finding, and the image provides some data for backup.

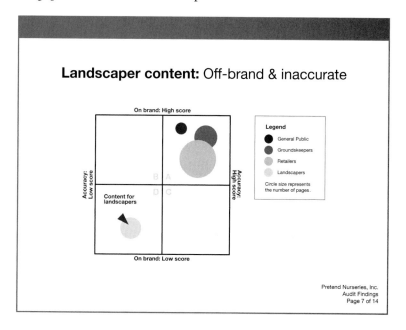

It's very likely that conducting an audit will earn you a huge promotion, a ton more money, and a year's vacation. Well, that might be a bit optimistic. At the very least, it will get people's attention. And once you have people's attention, you have the opportunity to present a business case for your next project or initiative.

BUT WAIT, THERE'S MORE

With a completed audit under your belt, you should have a clear understanding of the content you have. It's likely you have lots of ideas about what to do next. Why not jump right in?

Hold on there, chief.

There's more juicy info to be had about user needs, competitors, and the content team within your organization.

Next stop? Analysis.

6 ANALYSIS

CONTENT DOESN'T EXIST IN A VACUUM. There are forces—both from within your organization and from the outside world—that shape what your content is and what it could be. Business goals, resource constraints, user needs, and competitor activities are just a few things that influence your content in a big, big way.

To make effective recommendations about content, you need to analyze the wild, wide world in which your content lives. So, before jumping into strategy, take the time to ask pertinent, important questions about all the factors that impact your content's creation, maintenance, and ongoing success.

In this chapter, we'll discuss different aspects of ecosystem analysis, and why they're essential to your content strategy efforts:

- **Internal impact factors:** How does your organization impact your content?

- **External impact factors:** What effects do users, competitors, and influencers have?

- **Communicating the results:** How do you document and share what you've learned?

Please note that just because internal impact factors come first in this chapter doesn't mean you need to do them first. Want to start with external impact factors? Need to do external and internal simultaneously? Go right ahead. The choice is yours.

NO TIME OR BUDGET FOR ANALYSIS? FIND IT.

When you're constantly being asked to deliver projects in less time with fewer resources and smaller budgets, how can you possibly slow down for content-focused analysis?

The real question is … how can you not?

Analysis uncovers unrealized challenges, risks, and opportunities. With your analysis in hand, you can base your future recommendations on reality. And that's not just a good idea, it's crucial. It's a step you can't afford to skip.

BITE OFF ONLY WHAT YOU CAN CHEW

Analysis doesn't have to be some megalithic effort. Your analysis activities can be scaled according to project size and resource constraints. **Please note that we said scaled, not skipped.**

If you're short on time, figure out which activities and information are most valuable to your specific project. Just remember: Every hour you spend in analysis will likely save dozens, if not hundreds, of hours during content creation, delivery, and upkeep.

INTERNAL IMPACT FACTORS: LOOK DEEP WITHIN

Looking inside the organization is an easy place to start. After all, you (or members of your client team) work there. But whether you work for an organization directly or as a consultant, it's hard to convince people to do analysis on their own company. Why spend time, energy, and budget learning things they already know?

Chances are, nobody's ever sat down and taken a comprehensive look at the content's purpose, process, and policy. And, even if someone has, how long ago did it happen? **When internal analysis is ignored or out of date, entire strategies are built on un-researched assumptions and isolated opinions—costing everyone time and money.**

HOW DO YOU "DO" INTERNAL ANALYSIS?

The best way to conduct an internal analysis—by far—is to talk to people inside the organization. Sure, you can spend some time digging through documentation, but at some point, human interaction is required.

You can get perspectives from people in several ways, such as:

- **Interviews:** One-on-one discussions are a great way to get the real dirt. You're able to follow the interviewee's specific interests and ask lots of follow-up questions. As an added benefit, interviews are a great way to start a personal relationship and develop trust. That'll be helpful later, when you develop recommendations and try to implement them.

- **Group discussions:** Talking to several people at once will get you more general information than interviews. However, it's an efficient way to get information and help people learn about each other's perspectives at the same time. Be sure to keep groups to a manageable size. Fewer than eight people is probably best.

- **Questionnaires or surveys:** These aren't ideal, but they can help you gather information from large groups of people, and help them feel included. Questionnaires and surveys work particularly well if everyone you're surveying does the same job. (For example, a well-done email questionnaire to a group of sales reps could provide you with a lot of information about how they use content during sales calls.) Just be sure the questionnaires are short and easy to complete. It's also helpful if someone with authority encourages participation.

No matter what method you use, be sure to really listen to people—even if their perspective is different than the majority's. There is nearly always something you can learn from everyone.

Once you've completed your conversations, summarize the big themes and note discrepancies. You'll want to include your interview results when you share your research later. (It probably goes without saying, but be careful not to betray any confidential information when reporting your findings. Nothing kills trust like telling tales out of school.)

LISTENING: THE CONTENT STRATEGIST'S MOST IMPORTANT JOB

Brain Traffic's Erin Anderson says that when it comes right down to it, our most important job as content strategists isn't content strategy. It's listening.

This means the kind of listening that demands our active attention and participation. The kind that leaves us with the information we need to recommend truly smart, thoughtful content solutions. The kind that requires complete focus on the content challenge at hand.

Whether you're scoping a project, clarifying user goals, or managing rounds of client feedback, Erin suggests holding fast to a few rules for active listening:

1. **Act like a journalist.**

   "Open questions" start with "who," "what," "when," "where," "why," "how," "how much," etc. If we're only getting yes/no answers from a client, it means we're being lazy reporters. And it means our conversation can only scratch the surface in terms of uncovering user needs and business goals.

2. **Get comfortable with silence.**

   If a question we ask makes the interviewee pause or react emotionally, it's natural to want to lighten the mood. But jumping in to fill the silence can kill a potentially illuminating discussion. Uncomfortable silences often signal an imminent breakthrough or moment of truth. It's worth letting your interviewee collect his thoughts and respond candidly when he's ready.

3. **Ask silly questions.**

   We wouldn't be doing anyone a favor by pretending we have all the answers. More to the point, asking "stupid" questions quickly exposes the big, ugly, chronic content problems nobody wants to tackle. A good goal is to ask at least one such question in each client meeting.

4. **Check your work.**

   So we've done our job, asked our questions, and listened carefully to the answers. But only after we've agreed on the issues at hand can we proceed with a meaningful plan. That means organizing the resulting data into a document that can be discussed, aligned and signed off on, and used to guide the way forward.

FACTORS THAT MATTER

When you start peeking under the covers of your organization, it's easy to get overwhelmed. Seriously. It can be ugly in there. But you don't have to tackle everything at once. When you're designing your interview questions, start by focusing on these four topics:

- **Target audiences:** Who do you want to engage in conversation? Why? (We'll talk about *actual* users a little bit later.)
- **Messaging:** What do you want those target users to know, learn, or "get" from your content?
- **Channels:** What channels (on- and offline) are used to deliver content? How are they all connected? What is the business purpose of each one?
- **Workflow/Governance:** How is content created, maintained, and managed? Who's involved?

In our experience, when you have answers to these questions, everything else gets a lot clearer. And although they might sound easy, answering these questions is deceptively difficult. Even if you can answer them off the top of your head, it's likely that people in your organization will have different perspectives. And that's where the fun begins.

Let's take a closer look at the "big four."

Target audiences: Who are you trying to reach?

Who is your web content for, ideally? As you ask your stakeholders this question, people will have lots of different opinions. The marketers will say, "It's all about the customer." Human resources will want to please job seekers. Investor relations will want to talk to—surprise—the investors. This is to be expected. For right now, just find out as much as you can about each audience. Ask stakeholders to:

- Define their target audiences clearly. For example, ask, "When you say 'customers,' which are you referring to: prospective customers, existing customers, or both?"

- Describe why the audiences are important to them (the stakeholders) and to the business. It may seem obvious why an audience—like investors—is important, but hearing the stakeholder specifically answer this question can be pretty informative.

- Arrange the target audiences in order of importance to them *and* to the business (and if the lists are different, have them explain why).

Compile all of the information you gather in your analysis findings document so you can share it later. During the content strategy recommendations phase, you'll need to get everyone together and negotiate some priorities and parameters. (See *Chapter 8, Content.*)

Messaging: What are you saying?

"Messaging" is one of those words that means something different to everyone. To some, messaging is about creating specific words and phrases in an approved copy bank. To others, it means defining a "brand promise" or voice and tone (e.g., "We want to sound friendly but sophisticated.").

To us, messages are simply bits of information (thoughts or ideas). ***Messaging* is the art of deciding what information or ideas you want to give to—and get from—your users.** Needless to say, messaging is an important part of defining your content requirements. You can use messaging to:

- Prioritize content needs
- Keep content consistent (over media and time)
- Align content owners on content requirements

During your analysis, you don't have to define the messages you will use in your content going forward. But you do need to understand what messages exist in content today (whether it's on purpose or not) and how (or if) stakeholders would like messaging to change in the future.

If you're in a large organization, there might be multi-million dollar projects devoted to creating established messaging hierarchies (present and future). If you're in a smaller organization, a web project might be the first time anyone has really thought about messaging. Either way, you need to get input from all of the key stakeholders about what they want to say to their target audiences.

Then, when you create content strategy recommendations, you will work with the stakeholders to narrow the field of possibilities—and choose the right combination of messages for the content.

Channels: Everything's connected

A channel is a medium through which content is delivered. Users are likely going to use several channels (on- and offline) over the course of their relationship with you, so it's important that everything is consistent and complementary. That means all of the content creators in the organization, regardless of the channels they focus on, need to work together. The first step to that collaboration utopia is just identifying what's out there.

What channels exist?

Organizations are often stunned to realize how many content irons they have in the fire. It's not uncommon for a large organization to have hundreds of websites all pointing to each other with no master plan. And don't get us started on print materials or social media or mobile initiatives or SEO-focused content or … are you cringing yet? Because we are.

To get a handle on what exists, you can:

- **Talk to communications producers** (marketing, PR, advertising, technical communications, etc.) and find out what they have and how it's related to your content. For example, is someone creating a print brochure that will tell the user to go to your website for more information? If so, the website needs to have more information. Good to know.

- **Ask your friendly IT people for help** compiling a list of all the URLs the company owns and stats on the traffic to each one. Are all the URLs still active? Have any sites been ignored or forgotten? How much traffic goes from one site to another?

- **Follow the links** on your corporate website and see where they go.

- **Search for your organization** on search engines and social media sites—you might be surprised at what you find created by (and about) your organization.

Common channels you should watch for include:

- **Public website(s):** What are all of your organization's public websites? (There are likely more than you think.)

- **Social media activities:** Where do you have active accounts? What types of content are being shared among social media participants, and where?

- **Mobile:** Is there a mobile version of your website? Do you have proprietary applications delivering content to your mobile users?

- **Intranets/extranets:** Are there intranets/extranets associated with the organization that your users may access?

- **Public relations and awareness:** How does the PR team work? Are there other awareness campaigns or tactics? (For example, does your boss do a lot of public speaking?)

- **Print media:** Do you communicate to your users with brochures, spec sheets, or similar? If so, are users likely to see those materials before or after they see your web content? Do they refer to your project content?

- **Email campaigns:** Do you communicate regularly to your users via email? Will those emails link to your project content?

- **Advertisements/SEM:** Are there advertising campaigns currently underway? What about paid search placements? Do they link to your project content?

This undertaking, of course, is easier said than done in midsize to behemoth-size organizations. If you can't get the whole picture, start with your highest priority channel or area of focus. Find out what it is connected to. Repeat with the next priority channel when time and resources allow.

Once you know what exists, mapping everything out can help you (and your content partners) understand how things are interconnected. A map sheds light on how important it is not to publish, revise, or remove content without understanding what other sources may point to that content as a solution or reference for potential customers.

Here's a simple example. AwesomeCo is a growing software company. They're planning to redo their website, so they've created a channel map with the website as the focus.

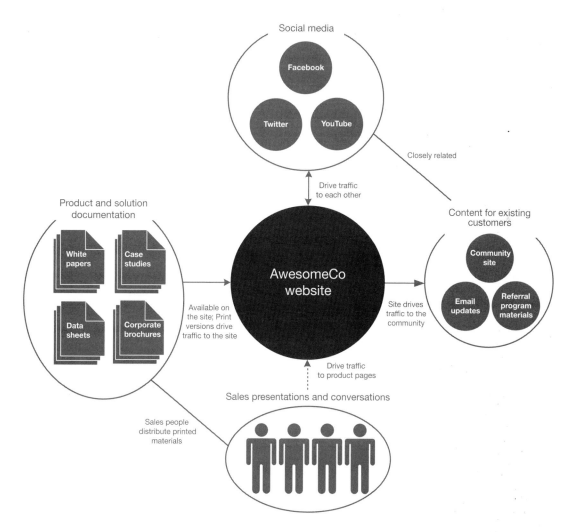

How do users (ideally) interact with each channel?

The next step is to define the role each content delivery channel plays in your target audiences' relationship with your organization. When you understand why (and when) the target users access each channel, you'll have a better grasp on what content belongs where.

One way to do this is to compare your channels to a "user lifecycle." A user lifecycle provides a step-by-step explanation of how the user relationship would work in an ideal situation. The most common lifecycles focus on a consumer purchase path (how we get a customer to buy something). But, you can also create lifecycles for other objectives, such as knowledge acquisition (how we get an audience to learn something) or loyalty (how we entice an audience to return to the content regularly). Check with your business strategy, communications, and marketing teams to see if any of these lifecycles have already been developed.

When you've established a lifecycle, you can see how your content delivery channels fit into the overall process by assigning each channel to one or more lifecycle steps.

In this example, AwesomeCo has already established a five-part lifecycle for clients:

- **Learn:** Prospective client hears about us for the first time.
- **Consider:** Client looks to see if we have the services they need.
- **Try:** Client decides whether the solution is a fit by looking at demos, case studies, and other documentation.
- **Buy:** Client makes a purchase decision and negotiates with sales representatives.
- **Use/Maintain:** Client uses software and requires support and maintenance.

Here's how the channels look plotted next to the lifecycle:

AwesomeCo: Client lifecycle comparison

Because AwesomeCo tailors each piece of software to the client's needs, the goal of channels such as the public website and print materials is to drive clients toward a negotiation with the sales team. But, because their primary prospect acquisition tactic is referrals, they also spend a significant amount of time on social media and content for existing clients.

When you take a close look at all of the channel connections and user relationships, you are able to better focus future content efforts—avoiding duplication and improving the overall user experience. And, that makes everyone—the business, users, and you—a whole lot happier.

Workflow and governance: How does content happen?

It seems like everyone has an opinion about web content, but no one is really sure whose job it is to assess requests and implement changes. So, it's best to find out who's involved and how the content process currently works.

Roles: Who's doing what? (And why?)

In most organizations, even small ones, roles that include responsibilities for web content are somewhat of a moving target … or, in some cases, an unsolved mystery.

There are more than a few people who may be involved with your content from concept to publication. Some people may play multiple roles. Here are a few examples:

- **Requesters** submit requests for web content to be created, updated, or removed.
- **Providers** are subject matter experts who own and manage source content—or who have the necessary information in their heads—that will be used by creators to develop web content.
- **Creators** are responsible for actually developing the content (text, graphics, audio, and video).
- **Reviewers/approvers** must be consulted about some or all of the content prior to its publication online. (*Note*: Not every reviewer will have the same clout—do your best to understand who needs to be involved and how.)
- **Publishers** get the content online, via coding, a content management system, a wiki, a blog, or other technical wizardry.

During your analysis, you need to find out who these people are. Which department do they work in, and who do they report to? What are their skill sets? Is content part of their job description or an afterthought in their already busy schedule? Are there interoffice politics involved that may affect content recommendations? This can be a tricky topic to navigate, especially in larger organizations. But, the answers to these questions are *essential* to understanding how the content process works today—and how you can get it to work better in the future.

Process: Tasks and timing

From request to publication to archiving (or not!), your organization has workflow and governance processes for getting "all things content" done. Even if these processes aren't standardized or documented, they exist.

Why is understanding processes so important? Because any changes to content will create changes to the processes. So, take time to know what you're messin' with.

Find out:

- What are the existing processes for planning, creating, translating, and maintaining content?
- Do they work differently for typical content updates versus emergencies?
- What parts work well? Which don't?
- Where are the bottlenecks and stopgaps?
- Who is overworked and who has capacity (and ability) to take on more?
- Are there tools—like style guides or templates—in place?
- How is content effectiveness measured, if at all?
- Is there anyone actually responsible for designing and overseeing content tasks?

Again, it can help to sketch out your findings by creating a current work-flow map.

AwesomeCo: Public website content workflow – Part 1: Creation

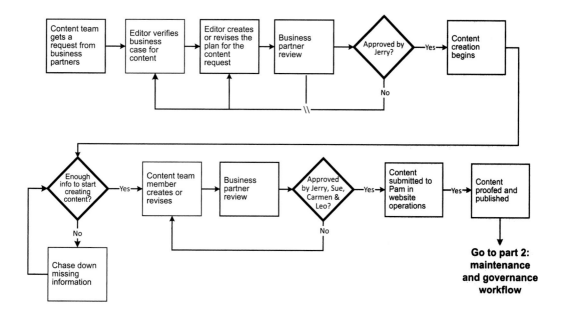

In most cases, documenting a workflow is an eye-opening experience for everyone involved. Who knew there were so many steps? Who knew the editors often need to chase down missing information from subject matter experts? Why are people in four different departments reviewing content before it goes live? No wonder people hate content.

Governance: What are the laws of the land?

While you're learning about content workflow, keep an eye out for governance activities. Try to find out:

- Who makes the decisions about content standards?
- How is content success measured?
- Are there content policies, standards, style guides, or other editorial tools in place?

There might not be any governance. Or every department in the organization might have its own rules. Either way, you need to know what's up.

Workflow and governance analysis helps your stakeholders understand the true scale of the investment (time and money) your organization makes in content. Which, in turn, leads to realistic expectations. Which then leads to workplace harmony, and probably world peace. (See *Chapter 9, People*.)

EXTERNAL IMPACT FACTORS: LOOK AROUND YOU

Knowing what the organization wants is important, but be careful not to fall victim to the "navel-gazing" syndrome. You know, the phenomenon where organizations spend so much time thinking about themselves, they forget there's a real world outside with the power to bring them down. You need to analyze the forces beyond your control that impact your content.

USERS: HERE THEY COME (OR GO)

Ah, users. You know, the whole problem with users is this whole "free will" thing: They show up, sign in, or download at their own discretion. You can't make them do anything they don't want to do. Their actions are *out of your control*. So inconvenient.

No matter how they find you, your users almost always have very specific goals and expectations. And if your content doesn't meet their expectations—and quickly—they will leave. Period.

Now, you may *think* you know what they want. This, of course, is silly. While you may be an expert about your product or service, you most certainly cannot read your users' minds. In order to really know what your users' goals are, you need to find a way to ask them. You also need to understand where they're coming from, who else they're talking to (competitors), what your audience segmentation is, and which messages will most likely convert and retain them.

User research: Who are these people, anyhow?

There are unlimited ways to get a good understanding of who your users are, what they want, and how they interact with you. In Colleen Jones' book, *Clout*, she discusses a wealth of ways to get more information about your users—their demographics, preferences, expectations, interests, and behaviors. Her list includes:

- **User interviews:** An in-depth, structured conversation with a user, usually conducted in person
- **Survey:** A series of multiple choice, fill-in-the-blank, and open-ended questions
- **Multivariate and A/B test:** A comparison of how different versions of important pages (such as product pages or landing pages) perform on your live website
- **Website analytics:** Detailed statistics about how visitors use your website
- **Social and reputation analytics:** Measurements of how users are talking about and referring to you on social networks
- **Search and keyword analytics:** Measurements of the words people use when they look for content through search engines such as Google (external search), and search on your website (internal search)
- **Contact analytics:** Measurements of why and how users contact you (by email, call, chat, etc.) and how they respond
- **Syndicated research:** Research conducted by an independent company or organization and often sponsored by several companies within an industry*

---

*This is an abbreviated list. For further details, see *Clout: The Art and Science of Influential Web Content.*

We'd also add:

- **Focus groups:** A moderated group discussion, where several users answer your questions en masse
- **Customer service analysis:** A survey, interview, or data analysis (where call center or support data is available) about most frequently asked questions, issues, and requests your customer service or sales people get from users

User research comes in many flavors and can work at all budget levels. If you've got the cash for intense studies in an official user lab, hooray! If not, you can try more do-it-yourself options, such as surveys or simply asking a few people what they think.

Website analytics: The perennial favorite

Web analytics is just one of the user research methods listed above, but analytics sure are popular. The ability to measure—with some precision—how people interact with our content has been one of the unique, revolutionary aspects of the Web. And it's so easy. The analytics software just creates the data on its own. Sort of.

Analytics, used well, can be a goldmine of information. But, they can also be extremely misleading. For example, just because a page gets little traffic doesn't necessarily mean users don't want to see it—they might not know it exists. Or, if your analytics system was not set up appropriately, all of the data could be skewed.

As Colleen Jones says, "Data is your eyes, not your brain." The data itself is not the outcome. The real value of analytics and other measurements is interpreting what they mean for the bigger picture: how your content is performing. So, work with your analytics team to understand your metrics. And remember: Analytics are only one source of information—it's a good idea to use several types of evaluation to get the full picture.

Usability testing: See your content in action

Even though content is often the number one thing that can make or break a user experience, usability testing—observing people while they interact with a product or site—often fails to consider it. And it should. As Angela

Colter (Electronic Ink) writes, "While usability testing watches what users do, not what they *say* they do, content testing determines what users understand, not what they *say* they understand."

There's nothing quite like sitting down and watching users interact with your content. Colter recommends using standard readability formulas, moderated usability tests, unmoderated usability testing, or a cloze test (a test that removes certain words from a sample of your text and asks users to fill in the missing words). The important thing is to find a way to test not only user behavior, but user *comprehension*.

If you're working on a project in which the usability testing falls outside of your jurisdiction, now is the time to make friends with colleagues on the design or UX team. Learn about other plans and processes for user testing. Find out if, how, and when you can collaborate. Work together to get the information you need.

COMPETITORS: THE OTHER GUYS

In order to make strategic recommendations that will set you apart from the crowd, you need to understand the competitive landscape. Now, many organizations make the mistake of going to their competitors' websites and freaking out because said competitor has x, y, and z content that *their* website doesn't. Inevitably, there's a fire drill called by someone whose main objectives are to "achieve parity" and "establish competitive advantage" by adding more content to your web properties.

Don't audit and analyze your competitors' websites with the idea that you need to keep up. Consider instead where you can create *true* competitive advantage. Nine times out of ten, this simply means optimizing your current content (in quality and structure); fixing your site search; and making smart, strategic decisions about what new content you'll add to the site—why, when, how, for whom, by who, and so on.

Chances are, your organization has already done some competitive research—which is a valuable place to start. But, general competitive research doesn't usually focus on content. Take another look at your competitors' content and consider the following questions:

How are competitors' websites organized?

By looking at how your competitors structure and label their websites, you will discover:

- Whether industry-standard labels have emerged. For example, if all your competitors are calling their technical support section "Support," you need to decide whether to stick with the standard or go with a more differentiated option.

- If there's a trend toward organizing similar content by audience, by target market, or by product or service type.

- Where you may be able to borrow intuitive, efficient taxonomies (ways content is organized, categorized, and structured) from websites that are clearly doing things right.

What topics are covered?

What are your competitors talking about? Again, this is not an exercise to determine what content you're missing. Your web content doesn't need to include every topic that every competitor includes. Instead, use this as an opportunity to identify where you can create differentiation. What *aren't* your competitors saying? What content does your user research demonstrate is most important?

What content formats are available?

Are your competitors featuring mostly text, or do they have podcasts and video? Do they prefer FAQs or contextual help? Is there a community forum or a review system where user-generated content is helping to inform other people's buying decisions? Are their employees blogging?

See how other organizations are supporting the user lifecycle with their web content types. Keep in mind any options that might be well suited to your target audiences, timeframe, internal resources, and budget.

What's their brand and messaging like?

You don't want to sound like all the other guys. In fact, you may find that all the other guys sound too marketing-y, too academic, or too technical; this provides you with a tremendous opportunity to stand apart from the crowd by creating content that reflects your unique brand and is clear.

Note things like key messaging, voice and tone, images, video production values, and so on. What are the brand attributes you'd assign to each competitor's content? Is the site's personality consistent page-to-page, or is it all over the map? And so on.

CASE STUDY SIZING UP THE COMPETITION

Laura Blaydon works at Manifest Digital, an independent interactive agency in Chicago, Illinois. This content veteran has some valuable advice for doing an in-depth competitive analysis as part of a multidisciplinary discovery process: Make sure you set aside plenty of time up front to uncover every detail you'll need before you get started.

Laura recently worked with a major insurance company that was trying to get a handle on the content their competitors were offering. Together the team went through these steps to define the focus and scope for their analysis:

- Select competitors for inclusion
- Determine evaluation criteria
- List content types/page types to be included
- Outline scoring method/model

They spent quite a bit of time defining what they would study and how they would study it. They came up with an impressive methodology for assessing content effectiveness. They only hit one snag: Laura's team had nearly finished collecting data when the client decided to add another competitor to the pool partway through the project.

Adding a new competitor didn't simply cost extra data collection time; it also threw the other steps into question. The team had to backtrack and be sure that the content types and scoring method would remain valid.

Looking back, Laura is glad that her team had so meticulously vetted their definitions and collection methods, which definitely set the project up for success. If they had been able to address the need for an additional competitor earlier in the process, that would have saved even more time and resources in the long run.

In the end, all the extra time was worthwhile. Their thorough competitive analysis revealed surprising discrepancies among competitors and important opportunities for Laura's client.

Where else are competitors active?

Try to find out what other web content initiatives your competitors have underway. Are they delivering sponsored or branded content on other websites or via social media channels? Have they launched content-driven advertising campaigns? Are they working on related websites that have their own brand identity but are really owned by your competitors? (For example, Johnson & Johnson owns BabyCenter.com.) They may be creating or curating content in places you belong, or launching mobile apps.

INFLUENCERS: THE POWER PLAYERS

What's more powerful than a website? Faster than an RSS feed? Leaps over your advertising tactics in a single bound? It's the "influencers": People and resources whose opinions inform and shape your customers' opinions of your organization.

Today's technology landscape provides countless ways to research organizations and products. And more than ever, people rely on multiple sources of information to form opinions about organizations. What are your customers' top influencers saying about you? Does your web content support, contradict, or include influencer content? Why? Why not?

Here are some influencers to consider. They may not all be relevant to your organization's products or services, but it's worthwhile to check out the ones that are:

- Trade journals and industry associations
- Analyst reports
- News media coverage and business magazines (online and offline)
- Television news and talk shows
- Online message boards and forums
- Consumer watch groups
- Bloggers and social media sites
- Social media recommendations sites (such as Angie's List, Guidestar, or del.icio.us)
- Celebrity speakers or figureheads
- Friends and family

CURRENT EVENTS AND TRENDS: CONSTANT VIGILANCE

Everything from a new social media site to swiftly changing governmental regulations can impact your final content recommendations. Be sure to keep an eye on:

- **Current events:** Political changes, the economy, natural disasters, etc. can all shape your content strategy and ongoing content maintenance needs.

- **Advances in technology:** New technology is introduced constantly—your content can be greatly impacted when new technologies such as devices (smartphones, tablets, etc.), programming languages, content management tools, or accessibility tools are released.

- **Trends and best practices:** Being a good content strategist or content professional means being a consummate content consumer. That means you always need to be on the lookout for new and interesting content practices that you can use in your own projects. As you go through your daily activities online, ask yourself questions like: Could I use this navigational technique on my site? Infographics are popular right now, are they appropriate for us?

COMMUNICATING THE RESULTS

To make the analysis phase really worthwhile, once you've finished, you need to present your key findings to all of the project stakeholders and get them to align on project objectives, assumptions, and risks based on a common level of knowledge.

In an analysis summary document, spell out everything you've learned, from business goals and internal requirements to user needs and competitive advantages. This document shouldn't include any recommendations for the future content. Its sole purpose is to ensure that everyone on the content team starts the content strategy process with the same information about the complex ecosystem your content lives in. This alignment is key to collaboration and buy-in later.

Your analysis summary document also will serve as a stellar reference guide for the project. It can help focus resources appropriately, prevent scope-creep, and identify opportunities. Finally, it helps the team remember where you started from and why early decisions were made.

MISSION DISCOVERY: COMPLETE

So. Here we are.

Your discovery phase is coming to a close. In *Chapter 4, Alignment,* you began the process of getting all of your stakeholders involved in the project. In *Chapter 5, Audit,* you did a deep-dive audit of your content. And, here in this chapter, you analyzed all the factors that have impact on your content.

And now?

You're ready to set your course for the future. It's strategy time.

(p.s. After all this, can you *believe* people are always waiting until the last minute to figure out their content? Seriously. Blows our minds.)

STRATEGY

Here it is. The moment you've been waiting for. It's time to put your content to work, to transform it into the business asset you've always known it could be.

7 CORE

CONTENT STRATEGY is a bit like going on a trip. If you've done your audit and analysis, you know where you're starting from. With alignment, you've ensured your travel companions are ready to go. But, before you start planning the specifics of your journey—you need to answer one extremely critical question: What's your destination?

Back in Chapter 3, we introduced the content strategy quad. Right in the middle of that bad boy is the *core strategy*. The core strategy is what connects all the other components of your content strategy together: It provides the all-necessary "guiding light" that keeps you moving in the right direction, no matter what might happen along the way.

In this chapter, we'll answer three questions:

- What is a core strategy?
- How do you develop and define a core strategy?
- What does a finished core strategy look like?

WHAT IS A CORE STRATEGY?

In any industry, things change constantly. Unfortunately, that means your content needs to change constantly to stay relevant. As a result, you may find yourself in constant content catch-up mode—always reacting to the next thing that comes down the pike and never seeming to make progress.

This is where your core strategy comes in. Again, your content strategy defines how an organization (or project) will use content to achieve its objectives and meet its user needs. The core strategy sets the long-term direction for all of your content-related initiatives—ensuring all activities, big or small, are working together toward the same magnificent future. Tactics might need to change, but your core strategy stays consistent. It helps you withstand the changes and keep moving forward.

An effective core strategy is:

- **Flexible:** It withstands the changing content environment, accommodating various tactics and team configurations.
- **Aspirational:** It's a stretch for the organization, focusing on what you want to become ideally (not what you can feasibly do).
- **Memorable:** It's an easily understandable concept that is used constantly to guide activities and decisions.
- **Motivational:** It's worthwhile and somewhat exciting—something people *want* to be a part of.
- **Inclusive:** It leaves room for a wide variety of individual and team contributions.

Defining your core strategy doesn't have to be a six-month odyssey that results in a 50-page document. Often, the majority of it can be hammered out in a series of workshops with your core project team ... but don't exclude your other stakeholders from the process altogether. Remember, content is a team sport. Whether you invite stakeholders to brainstorm with your core team or to react to work the team has already done, the key is to take their opinions into account. Your strategies will be better for it.

HOW DO YOU DEVELOP AND DEFINE A CORE STRATEGY?

Brain Traffic's Lee Thomas helps organizations define their core strategy using a concept he calls "Achieve-Be-Do." This approach helps answer critically important questions:

- **Achieve:** What does your content strategy need to accomplish (for the organization, for your industry, for your product, etc.)?
- **Be:** What "content product(s)" will we create? (In other words, what will we produce for our users/consumers? How will those content products be valuable to the users/consumers?)
- **Do:** What will the organization need to do to support the content effort?

Let's take a look at how this works.

FIRST, GET THE TACTICAL STUFF OUT OF THE WAY

When you first consider these questions, you'll probably find yourself jumping to tactics and solutions to immediate concerns. And that's fine. Go ahead. Get it all out. Brainstorm all the Achieve-Be-Do tactics and solutions you can.

Then ask yourself:

- What do these tactics have in common?
- What are the business or cultural themes underlying them?
- What about these tactics or immediate concerns prohibits us from doing better, cooler stuff?
- If I didn't have to do this stuff, what would I like to do with our content instead?
- If I had a magic wand, and I could instantly solve these problems, what would I do next?

THEN, GET ALL ASPIRATIONAL

Unlike plans, your core strategy shouldn't be based in today's reality. Achieving it should be a stretch for your organization, something to aspire to and build toward. So, just for this brief moment, don't think about what "is" today, what you need to do immediately, or what you think can realistically do. (We'll get back to that stuff in a bit.) For now, think big.

You'll know you're getting closer to your core strategy when your brainstormed ideas start to sound:

LESS LIKE ...	AND MORE LIKE ...
Provide information for law students.	We'll be THE reference resource for stressed-out law students—helping them become successful, ethical practicing attorneys.
Get on Twitter.	We'll meet our online customers wherever they are, providing them with the service they deserve, when they need it most.
The competitor has a mobile site. We should, too.	We'll develop a state-of-the-art content infrastructure that makes it easy for us to adapt to new device formats quickly.

Nobody gets motivated by "Let's try to keep up with the competitor" or "Let's make our product content slightly less crappy." Those may be the realities of your next few months, but they don't have to be your destiny. And, they certainly aren't your strategy.

DO NOT FEAR THE MAGIC LAYER

Content strategist Shelly Bowen refers to something she calls "The Magic Layer." For consultants, it's the place between research and deliverables. If you're inside an organization, it's the space between your research and your next promotion.

The magic layer is where all the unique and differentiating ideas—like the core strategy—come from. It's all about invention. And that can be scary.

In her blog post, "Just Make It Up, Already," Shelly says:

> This fear or resistance of invention—of making something up—is holding a lot of us back. It's as if we're looking for a book or resource or expert to point us to page 428, second paragraph, for specific and correct directions on what to do. (Then we can annotate it!)
>
> But how did that resource come up with the solution in the first place? They made it up. Sure, they tested it and shared it and revised it. They may even have come up with the idea from a range of sources and experiences. But some individual had to invent it and write it down.
>
> This business of "making it up" is [part of the Magic Layer] and I don't really talk about it to many people. For obvious reasons. Invention is welcomed in the art world, but within business strategy, it's much harder to accept.*

Do not fear the Magic Layer. You can do it. It's okay. And, what's more, you can't do content strategy without it.

---

*http://www.shellybowen.com/2011/10/magic-layer-invention/

WHAT DOES A FINISHED CORE STRATEGY LOOK LIKE?

There are no hard and fast rules for what a core strategy looks like. Contrary to popular belief, strategies don't have to be huge documents with "thud factor." In fact, at this stage of the game, big treatises are counterproductive. Nobody reads them, much less gets motivated by them.

Your core strategy can be as short as one sentence—as long as that sentence holds meaning for your whole team. It can be a graphic with a caption. We've even seen successful mnemonic devices and Top 10 lists a la David Letterman. The key here is short, memorable, and focused on your content. Feel free to make up your own format.

THE CORE STRATEGY STATEMENT: AN ANNOTATED SENTENCE

The *core strategy statement* is one of the tools we regularly use at Brain Traffic to communicate core strategies. We use this tool as a quick, memorable summary of all of the core strategy details we provide to our clients (often presented in a several-page document, which likely can't be easily repeated from memory).

Here's how it works. Remember diagramming sentences in grammar school? This is kind of the same, except you don't have to remember the differences between the participles. Instead of diagramming the parts of speech, you diagram a sentence that represents your strategy. Carefully select each word or phrase with your team, and then annotate the sentence to explain your selections.

This is an internal document. So, make sure the sentence sounds the way you would normally talk to your peers—not some formal rhetoric. You might even want to go through your stakeholder interview notes from the research phase to find effective phrases your stakeholders used themselves. Seeing their own words in print will up the ownership factor.

You might be surprised by the response to this scrappy little diagram. The key is to make it short, memorable, and meaningful.

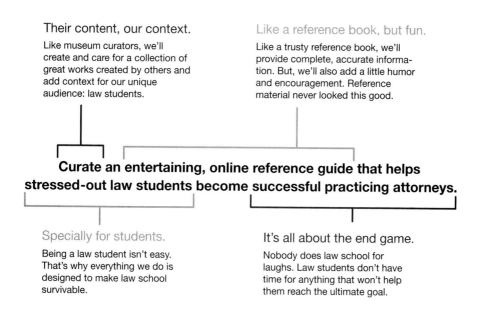

Their content, our context.

Like museum curators, we'll create and care for a collection of great works created by others and add context for our unique audience: law students.

Like a reference book, but fun.

Like a trusty reference book, we'll provide complete, accurate information. But, we'll also add a little humor and encouragement. Reference material never looked this good.

Curate an entertaining, online reference guide that helps stressed-out law students become successful practicing attorneys.

Specially for students.

Being a law student isn't easy. That's why everything we do is designed to make law school survivable.

It's all about the end game.

Nobody does law school for laughs. Law students don't have time for anything that won't help them reach the ultimate goal.

SO, WHAT'S THE PLAN?

We almost never present a core strategy without including a sneak preview into the first few steps of a tangible, executable action plan. The tactics in the plan that demonstrates how the strategy works in practice. We don't want to waste all that new-strategy energy and excitement. And neither do you. So let's keep rolling.

8 CONTENT

OKAY! CONTENT! This is going to be an easy, breezy chapter, because as we've been saying all along, content isn't really that hard to do!

Heh. Just jokin'. But it *will* be a fun chapter, because now we're going to explain how to define the **content components** of the content strategy quad. We'll walk you through the decisions you'll need to make, including:

- **Substance:** What content do you need and why?
- **Structure:** How will your content be prioritized, organized, formatted, and displayed?

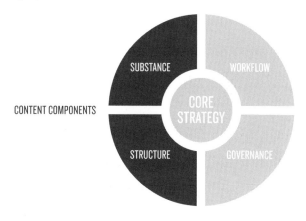

As you read through this (gigantic) chapter, please remember: When you make a choice about one component of the quad (like substance, for example), it very likely has impact on all three other components. **Connecting the *content* components and *people* components is one of the most important roles that content strategy plays in your organization.**

SUBSTANCE

Pop quiz: What should your content *do*? Okay, time's up. Answer: Your content must help you achieve your project objectives, your business goals, your user goals, and your long-term strategy. (Did you get it right? Great! Give yourself a pat on the back. Which is actually harder to do than one might think. Anyhow.)

In the past, you may have made decisions about your content by compiling colleague wish lists, polling your users, taking into consideration what content you already have online, and so on. These efforts resulted in a content list, which resulted in a site map, and so on. Although this may have been partially effective, you likely also ended up with a lot of stuff you didn't really need, after all.

Identifying what content you need is actually a pretty complicated process. There are lots of factors to consider, including:

- Audience
- Messaging
- Topics
- Purpose
- Voice and tone
- Sources

Let's take a look at each of these individually.

AUDIENCE: WHO ARE YOU TRYING TO REACH?

During analysis, you asked your stakeholders to identify and prioritize their target audiences. Go get that list now. We'll wait.

Obviously, stakeholders have different areas of focus. As a result, you probably have a list of several "equally high-priority audiences." For example,

Paul from PR wants to target the media; Juan from marketing wants to prioritize prospective customers; Mary in HR wants to reach job seekers, and so on.

While it's possible to create content that appeals to all of these audiences, it doesn't serve any of the users particularly well. **Your content will be much more effective and easy to manage if you set some parameters and priorities about who your content is for.**

Users: Get specific

Start by defining your user groups in detail. For example, if you say "customers," what do you actually mean? Do you mean prospective customers or existing customers? Do you mean customers for product line A or product line B? Do you mean soccer moms, punk rock fans, or soccer moms who are also punk rock fans?

Most importantly, define why punk-loving soccer moms are important to your organization and its goals. Why do you want to create content for them? What do you want them to do with your content?

Some organizations like to develop *personas*—fictional characters or archetypes that represent the user types. When done effectively, personas can help you define your users' characteristics clearly. But elaborate personas (for example, Margaret, 38, is a radiologist from Halifax, Nova Scotia, who likes rabbits and Neil Diamond …) aren't necessary. In fact, they can get a little distracting. A bulleted list of basic user attributes can work just as well.

When you have a clear definition of your target users, you have a better chance for creating content they'll actually use. You'll also make sure that everyone in your organization is talking about the same thing when they talk about a specific user group. There are lots of other benefits, too, but those two alone are worth the time and effort.

Priorities: Rank and file

Now comes the hard part: prioritizing your user groups for each content channel or web property you have (or want to have). Make a numbered list, starting with your first priority user as number 1. Then, continue down the list with the second priority, third, et cetera. It may be tempting to give two audiences the same ranking, but don't. No ties. Because of your stakeholders' multiple "top audiences," there will almost certainly be negotiation involved. Be prepared.

Additionally, ranking your users can identify gaps. For example, if you establish that "existing employees" are not a priority target audience for the public website—but they still need content for one reason or another—maybe an extranet or intranet is a good idea. Or, if you want to start a Twitter feed, but realize you don't know who it's really for, maybe you need to give the whole Twitter thing a little more thought.

Identifying and prioritizing your target users are the first steps in creating content that works for your users and your business. Not to mention, you'll avoid the countless, constant headaches that come with trying to be all things to all people. Bonus.

MESSAGING: WHAT YOU WANT YOUR USERS TO REMEMBER

As we explained in *Chapter 6, Analysis*, we define *messages* as bits of information (thoughts or ideas) you want the user to know and *messaging* as the art of deciding what information or ideas you want to give to (and get from) your users.

Messaging brings your *core strategy* to life. It helps you define what this specific web content needs to communicate in order to get you closer to your ultimate goal. It helps you prioritize content needs, keep content consistent, and align content owners on content requirements.

During analysis, we encouraged you to collect all the messages that exist in your content today, and what stakeholders would like added or changed. Now that you have a core strategy in place, it's time to prioritize those messages.

Defining a message hierarchy

The key to making messages valuable and understandable is putting them into a hierarchy that identifies your message priorities. For example, a simple messaging hierarchy would contain these components:

- **Primary message:** The single most important thing you want the user to know after viewing your content. This message is applicable to *all* of your audiences.

- **Secondary messages:** A group of key messages that support the primary message and provide context. These messages often highlight the things that are competitive advantages or differentiators. They may or may not be applicable to every single audience.

- **Details:** All of the various proof points behind the primary and secondary messages.

When you put all of these messages together, you've got a story.

Here's an easy way to picture this. Think of a magazine article about a business. The primary message is the title. The secondary messages are the subheads, and the details are all the sentences between the subheads.

Of course, when it comes to web content, the story's a lot more complicated. You'll have one major story (your primary message) and many, many subplots all linking to each other. Still, by identifying your main "stories," you'll have an easier time seeing the specific content you need to support, enhance, or expand on those stories (rather than random stuff you add "because you can").

Let's return to our friends at AwesomeCo, the up-and-coming software company who is building a corporate website. Their messaging hierarchy might look like this:

Primary message: AwesomeCo is the best-kept secret in business software.

Secondary messages:

- We don't sell products. We sell systems tailored to your needs.
- We use open source technology, so you're never held hostage to proprietary code.
- We work with 83 companies in the Fortune 100, new startups, and everyone in between.
- We don't do marketing; we're too busy making software. Our business comes from word of mouth.

Don't mistake messages for content

You don't have to spend days wordsmithing and agonizing over the exact phrasing and wording of messages, because they're not meant to be copy on your website; they're rarely shown to the user word for word. Instead, you'll interpret the messages for each audience and situation. In turn, the messages will influence the content you select and create. The primary message, for example, will be demonstrated with different content for different audiences throughout the site. And, you may never see the actual words.

For example, AwesomeCo's primary message might be interpreted on pages for different audiences like this:

Primary Message: AwesomeCo is the best-kept secret in business software.

Interpretations:

- **For client prospects:** We don't need to advertise because all our business comes from referrals.
- **For existing clients:** AwesomeCo "insiders" get special treatment with exclusive resources, discounts, and perks.
- **For investors:** AwesomeCo stock is a hidden gem that will soon become public knowledge, so act fast.

As you might guess, messaging doesn't always come easy. Remember trying to prioritize audiences? The very same people who had such different views on which audiences matter the most may very well have differing views of what's most important to communicate to users. So, like anything else that involves saying "no" to someone, defining and prioritizing messages will take some wrangling. Just fall back on those listening skills (see sidebar, page 72) and you'll do great. (Your wit, charm, and diplomacy will also serve you well. As always.)

TOPICS: THE SUBJECTS THAT MATTER

Okay! Now. What do you want to talk about?

Selecting topics isn't about brainstorming a list of interesting subjects. It's about narrowing the field—finding the right topic areas to meet your specific set of business requirements and user needs.

Your analysis helped identify what your audience wants. Your messaging communicates what information you'd like them to understand. Now, you can select topics to focus on what will fulfill both of your needs. So, basically:

Audience + Messaging = Topics

Take AwesomeCo's primary message: "AwesomeCo is the best-kept secret in business software." For the client prospects audience, topics might include: case studies of problems solved for customers, solutions and services, and their development process. Of course, topics may span more than one audience. Just be sure that each topic serves at least one audience. A video of the CEO's kid's soccer game? Yeah, not so much.

Topic maps

You can just make a list of all your topics and call it good. But, we really encourage you to go a step further and create a *topic map*. A topic map shows how your topics relate to each other. It can help expedite linking strategies, metadata, and CMS planning later. And if your website or content doesn't have a traditional navigation structure, a topic map goes from nice-to-have to necessary.

What you put on your topic map depends on how you plan on using it. In addition to showing how topics relate to each other, you can show how topics relate to user segments, messages, channels, or back-end infrastructure. A topic map can be as simple as this:

Or, a bit more complicated:

Process
Business consulting/analysis
Design
Development
Implementation
Testing
Integration
Maintenance

Case studies

Industries
Education
Energy and utilities
Financial services
Healthcare
Manufacturing
Media and entertainment
Retail
Science and technology
Travel and hospitality

Solutions/Specialities
Business intelligence
Business process outsourcing
Customer relationship management
Enterprise content management
Enterprise management
Financial management
Human capital management
Supply chain management
Small and mid-size organizations

About AwesomeCo
Philosophy
Innovation station
Leadership
Team

Media/Outreach
Press releases
Media kit
Blogger help
Industry outreach

Careers
Job listings
Benefits
Culture
Application process

Support
Knowledgebase entries
Lifetime support
Question line/chat
Community

Training
Classroom
Virtual classroom
Self-paced study
Certifications

Partners
OEMS
Software
Hardware
Hosting
Training

These are both pretty simplistic examples, but you get the idea. Once you figure out your topics, you'll be able to see how they relate to, inform, and impact each other.

PURPOSE: EVERY PIECE OF CONTENT NEEDS A JOB

When people talk about "content best practices," you often hear statements that sound like hard-and-fast rules, such as "web content should be short" or "everything should be three clicks from the home page." Unfortunately, it's not that simple.

Your content is a complex web of interconnected pieces of information—and each piece has a job to do. Just like you use a hammer and a wrench for different tasks, you use different kinds of content depending on the content's purpose.

Identifying a purpose for each piece of content can help you make informed decisions about what kinds of content you need. Here are a few examples of content purposes:

- **Persuade:** Get the user to make a decision in your favor—such as buy your products or agree with your opinion.

- **Inform:** Provide the user with information about a specific topic—for example, if a user wanted to learn about breeds of dogs or the fascinating life of Jessica Simpson.

- **Validate:** Give the user access to specific facts, so they can fact-check stuff like the year Columbus sailed the ocean blue (1492) or the dictionary definition of flibbertigibbet (a flighty, talkative person).

- **Instruct:** Teach the user how to do a task, like bake a pie, find a doctor, or set their Facebook privacy settings.

- **Entertain:** Help the user pass time. True entertainment content is rarely on a corporate site, but on a site like YouTube or Yahoo!, you'll see a lot of it. You know, cats playing the piano and all that.

It's worth noting that specific content may fulfill more than one purpose. Later in the process, when you're working with page tables (see page 125), knowing the purpose for each piece of content will help you determine what fits and what doesn't.

VOICE AND TONE: WATCH YOUR LANGUAGE

As a person, you have one voice. However, when you speak, your tone of voice changes depending on who you're talking to, what you're talking about, and the message you're trying to convey.

That's exactly how to think about your company's voice and tone when it comes to content. Your company has one brand voice that has a distinct personality, style, or point of view. That voice can take on different tones in different situations and for different purposes, all depending on your specific audience.

Defining voice

When you tackle defining your organization's voice, start by looking at any brand materials you have. The voice might already be defined for you. Consider how it feels, what values live behind it, the different media in which it might manifest. To explain it to content creators and others, select clear, recognizable adjectives. For example, if you're a financial services firm, your brand voice might be "trustworthy, straightforward, and authoritative." If you're a large university, your brand voice might be "aspirational, inclusive, and authentic."

Defining tone

Now, look back at the information you collected about your audiences. Combine that with what you know about the user's native voice and the objective of the specific website or channel content you are creating. Pick some words or phrases that describe how tone may shift for each audience. Funny? Enthusiastic? Calming? Helpful? To see this in action, check out the MailChimp case study on page 113.

It can help to look for example content from your existing content catalog, compare against your competitors, or review sites you (or your target users) like as examples.

Cultural differences

Just a quick note, here: Obviously, different cultures have different communication styles. Because we need to make sure our personality is understood in all our markets, our style may vary across countries—even different states and regions—to allow for cultural and linguistic differences. If necessary, get help defining a tone of voice that fits the cultural norms in each market.

SOURCE: WHERE YOUR CONTENT COMES FROM

The good thing is, there are several options for *acquiring* content to fulfill your content strategy. The bad news is, there's no truly easy way to go "get content" that will automatically make your content strategy succeed. **Even if you buy or license ready-made content, editorial oversight is still required** to ensure that co-created or third-party content meets your organization's brand guidelines, web standards, and user needs.

Let's look at the pros and cons of each option.

CASE STUDY ONE VOICE, MANY TONES

Kate Kiefer is a content curator at MailChimp, an email marketing service with a lovable chimp as its mascot. MailChimp is known for having a distinctive voice—one that strikes a perfect balance between playful and professional. But how can a large organization maintain a consistent voice when dozens of people are creating content?

Kate ran into this question as she worked to create a style guide for MailChimp. Initially she simply wanted to document grammar and other editorial considerations, but she soon discovered that writers needed a bit more. Kate and her team recognized that they also needed to create a voice and tone guide. Through collaborations with others, here's how they defined the MailChimp voice:

- Fun but not childish
- Clever but not silly
- Powerful but not complicated
- Smart but not stodgy
- Cool but not alienating
- Informal but not sloppy
- Helpful but not overbearing
- Expert but not bossy

These distinctions helped a lot. They captured the personality of the organization and gave writers a place to begin. But Kate discovered that defining MailChimp's voice was only the beginning.

Consider this: You're a MailChimp customer, reading a message about your successful email marketing campaign. You're thrilled with the results. If a cheerful cartoon monkey shows up on your screen to offer a verbal high five, it strikes exactly the right tone for your emotional state. But what if you've made a mistake, and your account is in danger of being shut down for spam violations? Suddenly a high-fiving monkey doesn't seem as charming.

That's the difference between voice and tone: a voice is a reflection of who we are, but tone is a reflection of the audience's emotional state. Just like a person, an organization has one voice. But we use that one voice to convey many tones, depending on the situation.

Check out the entire MailChimp voice and tone guide at http://voiceandtone.com/.

Original content

Content created by and for your organization is usually the most valuable kind of content: It's unique to you, it reflects your specific points of view, and it's communicated in your voice and tone. It's also the most expensive. But, when you take the time to really understand your audiences, create content specifically for and about them, and then deliver your content in formats that engage and motivate, you're delivering the kind of user experience that will bring people back for more.

To create original content, you (obviously) will need to do a lot of work collecting source material and generating new ideas. This can be time-intensive, so be ready to invest the necessary resources to make it work. (See *Chapter 9, People,* for more details.)

Co-created content

Big brands are making the most of high-profile bloggers, studios, podcasters, and other entities who are already in the business of creating content for an engaged audience or subscriber base. And that's smart.

If you're a food company, consider reaching out to popular food bloggers and hiring them to create content for your brand, either on your website or another sponsored channel. If you're a city or state visitors' bureau, partner with local photographers who will regularly upload photos to an online photo album featuring the best of your area. While you do give up some control of the content being generated with this approach, you're gaining built-in audiences, unique perspectives that can complement your brand strategies, and the opportunity to experiment with a wide range of content types, often for less time and money than would otherwise be involved.

Aggregated Content

There are also ways to collect content created elsewhere. One way is to automatically *aggregate* content from other websites or sources (which, of course, must be accurately credited). This can be accomplished in several ways. For example, you can pull content with an RSS feed, which automatically collects content from the websites or feeds you subscribe to. You could also create search algorithms, which pull content based on specific keywords or phrases.

There are a range of risks that come with taking this approach—everything from dumping too much content on your users that ultimately gets ignored to unknowingly publishing something that gets your organization in trouble. One of the more important risks, here, is that content is being published or linked to from your organization without any sort of qualitative review. Yes, the tools provide a filter of sorts, bringing in content they calculate to be of some worth. However, you're making a big assumption, based on subscription choices and keywords, that content will have relevancy and context for your audience. If it doesn't, you'll lose their attention and, potentially, their trust.

Curated content

Another way (and, for us, the preferred way) to collect content is to have someone research and *curate* content with an editorial point of view. Social media consultant Beth Kanter writes:

> Content curation is the process of sorting through the vast amounts of content on the web and presenting it in a meaningful and organized way around a specific theme. The work involves sifting, sorting, arranging, and publishing information. A content curator cherry picks the best content that is important and relevant to share with their community. It isn't unlike what a museum curator does to produce an exhibition: They identify the theme, they provide the context, they decide which paintings to hang on the wall, how they should be annotated, and how they should be displayed for the public.*

Please note that content curation is *not* the same as asking users to provide content reviews or ratings. Simply asking your users to rate your web content does not ensure that the most relevant, valuable content will be surfaced; overall ratings can be seriously skewed by just a few active (and opinionated) users. It's a way to *surface* content, but it's not curating it.

---

*http://www.bethkanter.org/content-curation-101/

Licensed content

If your content strategy includes offering a deeper library of online resources than you have the infrastructure to create, you may choose to license content created by a third-party publisher. (In this instance, it would also be the content strategist's responsibility to research, review, and recommend third-party content providers.)

Articles, images, audio, and video are all widely available for licensing online. Again, you may be risking brand dilution by offering generic content to your online users. However, this is a hugely popular (albeit questionably successful) option for a wide range of industry websites. For example, health insurers license content from WebMD, Staywell, the Harvard Medical School, and more.

Don't forget that licensed content still requires research and oversight. You'll also need to decide if you're just going to publish everything or manually curate it for your audiences.

User-generated content

Another way to source content is to invite users to create it themselves. For example, you may launch a community forum focused on product support, anticipating that users will essentially create "help" content for each other. Or you may invite users to create their own content as part of a brand campaign. If you choose the user-generated content route, be forewarned: without proper planning and oversight, these tactics can go awry. Case in point: An SUV manufacturer once invited their users to co-create commercials promoting a new SUV model. The campaign backfired when environmentalists stormed the virtual gates, creating commercials that damned SUVs as gas-guzzling, nature-killing, road-hogging beasts.

No matter what, don't just dive in to user-generated content tactics. Plan, test, measure, respond. Just because it works beautifully for some brands, doesn't mean it will for yours. Proceed with caution.

FINAL NOTE: YOU CAN'T ALWAYS HAVE (ALL OF) WHAT YOU WANT

Now you have your messages, topics, formats, and sources nailed down— great! Let's do this thing! Let's make some content!

Whoa, there. It's tempting to jump right in and start creating or collecting content just so you have something to show your boss or client. "See? We're out there, doing stuff!" But trust us: that is the path to suffering and doom. Over the years, we've seen it again and again: Organizations commit to an amount of content they simply can't sustain. They launch websites with unfinished or subpar content no one really had time to generate in the first place, let alone pay attention to once it went live. They create newsrooms and blogs that languish after only a few months. They start YouTube channels, but aren't sure what to broadcast (except commercials).

So, when the content you want is too much content for your resources to create and maintain—at least immediately—how do you prioritize what content gets done or done first? Brain Traffic's Lee Thomas has developed the following criteria:

- **Requirements:** Is the content required for some reason (legally, politically, for funding, etc.)?

- **Reach:** Which audiences is the content likely to reach, both today and in the future? How big are those audiences?

- **Relevance:** How important and interesting is the content to users? (The answer is likely to affect reach.)

- **Richness:** How valuable or unique are we able to make this content?

- **Revenue:** How will the content affect site revenue-generating activities (actual product sales, ad sales, etc.)?

Most of these criteria are somewhat subjective. It can be helpful to create a scorecard, where each topic, piece of content, or content category is given a score (on a scale of 1–5) for each of the other four "R"s. The content with the highest overall score stays, the lowest scoring content goes. The cut-off, which is somewhere in the middle, is defined by your timeline, budget, or resources.

Okay! Substance ... BAM. Done. Moving on to ... structure! (Insert sound of party horns.)

STRUCTURE

How will your website or other web content be structured? How does the navigation work? What pages live where? What content goes where, or on what page? How do things link together? What elements are on every page of the website?

My, you ask a lot of questions. It appears that you're ready to take on your next big challenge: structure.

WHOSE JOB IS IT, ANYWAY?

Figuring out how your content will be structured might sound like a job for an information architect (IA) or a user experience (UX) designer. And sometimes, it is. But sometimes content strategists consider creating a sitemap and wireframes to be part of their job. Some want nothing to do with it, preferring to focus on core strategy, workflow development, or editorial considerations. Sometimes the content strategist, an IA, and a UX designer all work together. Sometimes it's all the same person. **It really doesn't matter what your title is. Someone just needs to get the content work done.**

Another angle: IAs frequently focus on structure and functionality, not the overall story and page-by-page content details that will be housed (or powered) by that structure. So, **if you're doing a content strategy, and the information architecture is being done by someone else, you probably still have structural work to do.** If you own the content, you'll need to be a part of all IA documentation reviews to ensure that it meets content requirements.

WHAT DO YOU NEED TO DO?

To figure out how content should be prioritized, organized, formatted, and displayed, you'll have to make a lot of decisions. There are high-level decisions (What channel should we use?), decisions about minute details (How will we label that web page?), and everything in between. Here are just a few of the elements you'll need to consider:

Channels, platforms, and formats

At some point, you need to decide where you want to make your content available. That means you'll need to choose channels, platforms, and formats.

- *Channel* is the place or service through which you are communicating with your users. Examples: email, websites, SMS.
- *Platform* is the technology upon which you build your content or service in order to deliver or exchange content. Examples: content management system, mobile technology.
- *Format* is the way in which information is presented. Examples: text, audio, video, or images.

The primary question is, how can we get the right content, to the right person, at the right time, and in the right place? These decisions, like so many others, are not the sacred domain of the content strategist. But, when the time comes, here are some key content-focused questions to bring to the table:

- **What are the best formats to communicate (and demonstrate) your key messages?** For example, if you're a tool manufacturer, and you target the home do-it-yourself market, you may want to invest in a series of how-to articles focusing on home projects. It also might be smart to produce a video series showing how to do those same projects step-by-step.
- **Are these formats achievable?** It's easy to brainstorm great ideas, but they're useless unless they're workable. Do you have the time and resources to create a video series? If you decide on a weekly podcast, can you commit the time to prepare for the podcast, record, edit, and publish it?
- **Where are your audiences?** We talked about channels in *Chapter 6, Analysis*. Look back at your user research and determine which channels will be most effective. Think about where your users are, who they're interacting with, what they use those channels for, and so on.
- **How "portable" should your content be?** Users love to share content—they link to it, email it, embed it in their blogs. Will your content formats encourage or discourage this sharing? Are you comfortable letting your content "be free," or are there copyright or legal considerations that prohibit it?

A brief note about social media: "Social media" is plural for "social medium"; that means social websites and services are channels you use to deliver content to and receive content from your audiences. Is your CEO blogging? She's creating content. Is your intern tweeting? Content. Do you have a Facebook page that you're updating now and again? Content.

Here's another thing to consider: Just because you know where your audiences are doesn't necessarily mean it's a good place to talk to them. Case in point, take Facebook. Brands have jumped at the opportunity to build a presence on Facebook. Some of them have been quite successful. But many of them are out of place and generally ignored. Do I really want to become a fan of my neighborhood plumber on Facebook? No. I do not. I am too busy taking the "Which Star Wars Character Are You?" quiz and arguing with my mother on her profile wall.

Don't waste time delivering content where your audiences don't actually want you to be. Get their permission. Be supportive, not interruptive. Be persuasive, not overly persistent. Meet them in the middle.

Navigation and nomenclature

When users get to a website or similar channel, they need to be able to find the content they need quickly. That's why navigation and nomenclature are so important.

Nomenclature is the task of identifying which labels will be assigned to different components of a website. A *navigation system* defines how all of those labels work together to guide the user around the site.

Navigation comes in many different formats, from the traditional tree-like structure (with the home page at the top, main categories underneath the home page, and detailed content pages nested beneath the categories) to cloud-based sites with no permanent navigational features at all. What you choose depends on what the content needs to accomplish and for whom.

Nomenclature is necessary—not only for navigational menus but also for content modules (for example, the label for a sidebar on a web page). When choosing labels, it's important to:

- Keep an eye on how labels might support key messages
- Ensure context, consistency, and clarity at every level of required labeling
- Make sure, above all else, that the labels are intuitive to end users

Links

Part of your job may be to recommend how and when certain links will appear on the page (or as a specific module). As you think through this, consider that links can, for example:

- Drive users to tasks that support fulfillment of business objectives
- Steer users toward additional, related information that may support their decision-making processes
- Offer relevant pieces of information that will further engage the user in your brand experience
- Encourage users to join an online community, participate in a social media channel, or comment on a blog

Be sure to call out where links should appear, under which circumstances they should appear, how they should be written, and any consistent calls to action.

Microcopy

Microcopy is copy you probably don't even notice when you're using a website. It appears in menus and next to form fields. It can act as signposts throughout a website, so you can keep track of where you are. It gives instructions, alerts you to errors, even congratulates you when you've completed a task.

These little words have a big impact on your user experience. Joshua Porter, director of user experience at HubSpot, has written extensively on the power of microcopy. He writes:

> Microcopy is extremely contextual ... that's why it's so valuable. It answers a very specific question people have and speaks to their concerns right on the spot. And because it's so contextual, microcopy isn't always obvious. Sometimes you have to hunt to find the right words.*

Microcopy is often a focus in usability tests. As a content strategist, you probably can help out with some of this writing and evaluation. Ask the IA or interaction designer if you can sit in on the tests, or if they'd like your assistance early in the process.

---

*http://bokardo.com/archives/writing-microcopy/

What you should definitely do is collect requirements for microcopy—such as error messages or inline help text (that's the text that appears right in your screen when you click or hover over a link or object). Record them in a specific document, so that you can hand it over to a writer, or at least have it for reference during final content quality analysis (QA).

PREPARING CONTENT FOR THE FUTURE

It's difficult to get a handle on structural considerations when things seem to change constantly. Karen McGrane has spoken extensively on the topic of adaptive content. Here's what she has to say:

> For years now, organizations have been trying to retrofit their print content and digital documents into a web-based format: web pages published and managed by a web content management system (WCMS). Just as the old document model broke down when the Web arrived, the web page model is going to break down in the years to come, as we confront a future of multiple devices and platforms.

> If we're going to survive and thrive in the future, we need to start thinking about content as something that lives beyond a particular publishing platform. We can't just imagine how content will appear in a particular document or page or screen. Instead, we have to structure our content for reuse.

> Now, structured content isn't new, but it's always been positioned as a technology problem, the province of arcane acronyms and competing technical standards. But this isn't a technology problem; it's a strategy problem. What are the essential content objects we deal with? What metadata do we need to organize them effectively? What are the rules that our business has around them? If you can't answer those questions at that level, you're going to be caught off guard when the latest and greatest device or platform is introduced.

> Starting now, we need to finally separate content and form. Unless we really sit down and address our core content challenges—what we publish, why, who's responsible for it, and how we know if it's working—we're going to remain stuck where we are today: pinballing madly between devices and platforms, without any coherent long-term strategy.

Metadata and tagging

Metadata is "data about data." It's the specific words, numbers, and any other data that's assigned to different kinds of content—pages, modules, products, and so on. Metadata makes content findable, portable, and adaptive to different platforms. It's part of what web search engines look for in order to recognize and categorize content for their search results. It's what defines the results that come up when we use our internal site search engines. Metadata can also handle the organization and display of the content, along with links between the content.

As you can see, metadata is a big, unwieldy topic. But, with new channels and platforms being introduced every few months, it's more important than ever to consider metadata as part of structural recommendations. You should ensure that metadata:

- Accurately reflects the content substance
- Has attributes that will organize the content in an intuitive way
- Is consistent across content types and topics

In general, don't be afraid to dig into the details behind the scenes. These words and concepts might be unfamiliar to you, but once you understand the basics, you'll quickly recognize the power and potential of metadata.

WHAT TOOLS CAN HELP?

For more than a decade, "good" websites followed a common structure using the traditional tree-like navigation. As a result, some of web development's most recognized documentation tools were developed to design these sites.

Sitemaps

The *sitemap* is the most popular structural tool of all. A sitemap is a useful tool, no doubt; but sometimes, they fail to capture or communicate even the most basic content requirements.

Take, for example, the page stack—a stack of boxes that means "a bunch of other pages go here." Here's what it looks like:

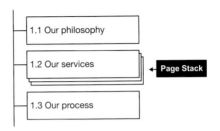

In his book *Don't Make Me Think*, Steve Krug describes page stacks as a smoke-and-mirrors way of abdicating responsibility for what actually happens after the first few levels of navigation. Krug says that, with page stacks, the IA is basically telling project stakeholders, "… and then the MAGIC happens!"

Page stacks are fine if the sitemap comes part-and-parcel with detailed recommendations about content. If it doesn't, the content owners are stuck with no direction, no context, and no idea what should actually go on those mysteriously stacked pages. We'll talk about how to avoid this problem later in the chapter.

Wireframes

In most IA documentation, page- or component-level content requirements are captured in *wireframes* (which are similar to architectural blueprints) or a *prototype* (a functioning version of a few pages of your website or web content components).

These tools can very accurately and effectively document content requirements for the pages they show. But, there are a few problems with them, too.

First, typical wireframes and prototypes show only a few "representative" pages of the website. (Obviously, it wouldn't be cost- or time-efficient to do them for every page.)

Second, there's some seriously important information about the content itself that's missing. To close the gap, there is another layer of "design," which considers how content—defined and driven by messaging, business objectives, and user goals—will receive the attention it deserves, at the right time in the project process.

Page tables

In order to take sitemaps and page templates to the next level, the level at which key content recommendations may be identified and explained, we need a third document, called a *page table*.

The page table tells you everything you need to know about the content on a specific website page (or content module): the content objective, key messages, specific content recommendations, source content quality, and requirements for how to create and maintain the content.

Here's an example of a page table:

4.1 Classroom Training

Page objective: Familiarize prospective clients with our classroom training offering and help existing clients choose between training options.
Source content: Training handbook
Phase: 1 (Launch)
SME/Content owner: Jane Fisher, training manager

Page Title	Classroom Training: Getting you up to speed
Priority 1 content Main content	Present an overview of the classroom training program and its benefits: • Tailored to each client organization and audience • On-site at the organization's location(s) • Training team includes experienced educators and programmers/technologists • Talk about the mix of lecture, exercises, and activities
	Assets: Image of the classroom
Priority 2 content Virtual classroom	Discuss how the virtual classroom brings the classroom experience to remote employees. Links to the Virtual Classroom page [Link to 4.2]
	Assets: Screen grab
Priority 3 content Ongoing support	Talk about how training continues throughout life of the product via our support services. Links to the Support section [Link to 5.0]
	Assets: None

- **Content creation implementation:** The source content is not public facing. The content will need to be edited significantly.
- **Maintenance frequency:** May need to be updated bi-annually after our corporate retreats.
- **Outstanding questions/risks:** None

Page tables are easy for stakeholders to edit and change, which is critical when there are tons of pages to review. And, for writers, page tables are pure gold: Having all of the source content locations, content owners and reviewers, message priorities, specific topics, and more right there on one page—before they start writing!—is every writer's dream come true.

When page tables aren't enough … or too much

On a website with hundreds, thousands, or hundreds of thousands of pages, it's neither cost-effective nor time-efficient to create a page table for every single piece of content. Sites of this magnitude include:

- **E-commerce sites:** mostly product descriptions
- **Encyclopedic sites:** sites that offer thousands of articles, indexed by topic
- **News sites:** articles and other content artifacts (images, audio, video) that are typically archived both by date and topic

In these cases, you can create a content requirements template (formatted like a page table) for all pages that have the *exact* same purpose and use. Not "sort of similar" pages or components. *Exactly* similar, like a press release, a product description, or a specific type of article.

Regardless of website size, all content recommendations need to *somehow* be documented to assist with content creation, maintenance, and migration tasks.

KEEP UP THE GOOD WORK

There it is. Useful, usable content that's valuable both to your audiences and your organization. The stuff you need to succeed.

You'll notice, however, that the book isn't over yet. While substance and structure are essential to a successful content strategy, good content itself isn't enough. You need processes, procedures, policies, and—of course—the people who make it all happen. There's an entire lifecycle to consider and plan for.

Let's get to it.

9 PEOPLE

YOU KNOW WHAT'S GREAT about the Web? There's always room for more content. And, thanks to the magic of distributed publishing, anyone can do it! Your website can just *magically expand* to include everyone's everything. And if stuff starts to get a little disorganized on your main site? Just get a different URL and call it a "microsite"!

Soooo ... how's that working out for you? Not so swell? Believe it or not, it's often not the content, itself, that's the problem. In this chapter, we'll focus on the **people components** of the content strategy quad:

- **Workflow:** What processes, tools, and human resources are required for content initiatives to launch successfully and maintain ongoing quality?

- **Governance:** How are key decisions about content and content strategy made? How are changes initiated and communicated?

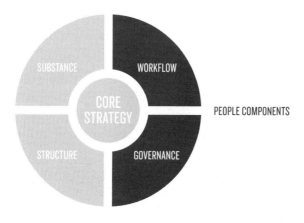

PEOPLE COMPONENTS

Although they're two different words with two different meanings, work-flow and governance are not easily separated. If you have workflow defined but no real standards or oversight to guide the people involved, it's already broken. Similarly, if you have all sorts of policies and people in charge but no process for implementation, then what's the point?

In this chapter, we'll talk about:

- Defining ownership and roles
- Designing content processes
- Documenting your processes
- Making it all happen

Whether you need totally new processes, roles, and tools or you just need to refine what's already in place, by documenting workflow and governance, you'll have a very clear vision of how, when, and by whom the work will get done. And, with better processes and more clearly defined roles, people will be much better prepared (and, likely, happier) when it comes to creating and caring for content.

DEFINING OWNERSHIP AND ROLES

So, this content. Whose job is it? Who's responsible? Who owns it?

It's safe to bet that there are lots of different people responsible for different aspects of your content and content processes. From requests to creation to publication, there can be all kinds of cooks in the kitchen. But, is anyone clear on who's really doing what? If not, you're going to end up with dupli-cate tasks, unclear authority, and a general lack of quality control.

It's critical for each person to know what their role is and how it fits into the larger content process. This is why defining ownership and roles is one of the most important aspects of workflow and governance.

Let's spend the next several pages taking a good, close look at all the differ-ent ways content ownership and roles might be defined and assumed.

BUSINESS UNITS: OWNERSHIP AT A MACRO LEVEL

There isn't one typical place for content to live within an organization. It is often shared between several departments or business units. So, who should have the final say about your website content?

It might seem easy to immediately disqualify, say, the CMS team, by saying that techies shouldn't be in charge of content. But, aren't they the ones typically responsible for publishing and archiving the content? That's sort of important. Often, they're also the folks who end up (by default) writing the metadata that makes your content findable, both by external search engines and your own site's engine. These things matter.

Maybe brand and marketing should take a back seat. Except, you know, they probably want input over little things like brand voice, messaging, style guide considerations, hierarchy of information, calls to action … right.

How about the web strategy team? Can they let go of ownership? Maybe content isn't that important to a successful user experience. Oh. Wait. It is.

And finally, the product/service SMEs, who probably are tasked with reviewing (or even writing) web content, on top of the 18 million other things they're supposed to be doing. We sort of need their input to make sure things are accurate and up to date.

Content needs a home

There's no denying that shared ownership is messy. That's why, ideally, content needs a place of its own—a home base that facilitates cross-team collaboration wherever content is involved:

Even if you can't create an entirely new business unit for content strategy—or you can't right away—you can designate a person or several people to have content strategy as part of their job description(s). And give those people latitude to be envoys to other business units. Content strategy ambassadors, if you will. That will help you ensure all of the business units understand each other and collaborate. Really, it can happen.

INDIVIDUALS: THE RESPONSIBLE PARTIES

No matter how the business units are set up, behind every thriving content project, there is an army of individuals keeping the content functional and fresh. The number of individuals, and the specific roles they play, varies by organization.

In addition to content strategists (see job description in *Chapter 3, Solution*), let's discuss some of the common roles you may want to consider for your content team.

Note: **These roles do not need to be job titles; they are areas of responsibility.** One person may fulfill several of these roles at once, and/or there may be several people with the same role. It all depends on your situation.

Web editor-in-chief

A web editor-in-chief helps to establish and enforce all web content policies, standards, and guidelines. Depending on the scale of web properties and initiatives, the editor-in-chief may serve either in an executive function—largely to oversee teams of web editors, and to facilitate their interaction with other business units and web contributors—or in an editorial function, working directly with web writers to ensure content quality and accuracy.

This is the person who is ultimately responsible for setting and communicating standards that will shape your web content, whether on your corporate website, your intranet, in social media, or anywhere else your company distributes content on the Web.

The editor-in-chief may also be responsible for the education and professional growth of content creators. He may also take the lead on educating requesters, providers, and reviewers/approvers on what your web content standards and processes are, and how they can expect to engage with creators and publishers.

Additionally, the editor-in-chief should be a key stakeholder in any content strategy initiative. No one will be closer to your organization's web content, and no one will be more deeply invested in its constant improvement.

Finally, if anyone is going to be familiar with the day-to-day challenges of dealing with web content, it will be your editor-in-chief. This person should weigh in on decisions like resource planning and management, content management technology purchases, and other operational considerations.

A web editor-in-chief:

- Sets and communicates web content standards
- Motivates and develops the staff
- Participates in web strategic planning
- Facilitates web content planning
- Participates in web operational planning
- May help make the business case for content
- Is empowered to say "no"

Web manager or editor

Web editors plan and oversee the publication of content. This may involve writing original copy, or coordinating and editing contributions from others. The web editor also maintains the web editorial calendar and maintenance plan. Although the role is usually mostly journalistic, it may also require technical skills and strategic planning abilities.

This role is necessary to maintain content quality, consistency, and relevance on your website. The web editor functions as a gatekeeper, and ensures new content is consistent with site strategy and relevant to users. The larger your website, the more web editors you will likely need.

A web manager or editor:

- Sets guidelines for the editorial tone, style, and voice of content
- Establishes a style guide and editorial procedures
- Oversees the development of content
- Develops and oversees the web editorial calendar
- Owns and facilitates the maintenance plan

Content creator

The content creator is responsible for producing accurate, compelling text that clearly conveys the required messages to the target audience and supports your content strategy objectives.

Because the bulk of the content on the Web is text, most content creators are writers. However, creators may also need to create assets such as images, diagrams, sound, or video, and provide appropriate captions for them. You may have separate content creators for text and other types of content—or one person may source or create all of them.

The content creator may also be responsible for providing metadata, such as keywords and a short description, to accompany each piece of content.

Content creators:

- Develop all required content (text, video, images, etc.)
- Work to enhance, edit, and reformat legacy and newly created web copy to conform to web writing best practices
- Ensure all content conforms to your web SEO requirements and best practices

Sourcing manager or curator

Although it might sound easy to buy or otherwise use content created by another organization, when done well, sourcing content can be a full-time job. Sourcing managers or curators are similar to web editors, except they're responsible for aggregating or curating content.

They identify appropriate content/content providers and work with the procurement department to negotiate contracts. Curators serve as the primary contact for content providers at all phases of the relationship—from set up to retirement.

A sourcing manager or curator:

- Sets guidelines for content selection and purchase
- Manages the contract renewal process
- Establishes a checklist of ideal content qualities (tone, topic, etc.)
- Adds commentary or context to the content, if necessary
- Develops and oversees the editorial calendar and maintenance plan

Search engine optimization (SEO) specialist

An SEO specialist analyzes your website's business objectives, content, and intended audiences in order to figure out which SEO strategies will win prominent listings in the results pages of web search engines.

This person should collaborate closely with web editors and writers to ensure keywords and phrases are incorporated into the site content. She should also be in touch with your development team to ensure technical implementation of web pages or content modules isn't interfering with SEO efforts.

SEO techniques change frequently, so a large part of the SEO specialist's job involves research, self-study, and reading in order to stay abreast of developments.

SEO specialists:

- Look for ways to improve and track SEO performance
- Identify appropriate keywords based on research and business goals
- Educate content creators and editors on search engine optimization

- Ensure the appropriate keywords are incorporated into content in accordance with SEO best practices
- Review keywords and keyword placement, as part of the content maintenance process

Subject matter expert (SME)

Throughout your organization, there are people who have knowledge on specific topics that they want to convey to your audiences. From marketing and branding to product development and operations, these subject matter experts may be the business owners for the content, or just the super smart people whose insight you need to get the content right. Depending on their role, subject matter experts may:

- Collaborate with the web editor on content planning and prioritization
- Represent their group's interests in the high-level conversations about content planning, creation guidelines, content resources, site organization, and more
- Review and approve major content launches
- Act as a content source, providing the information others need to create a piece of content, and reviewing the finished content product for accuracy and tone
- Act as a content creator, authoring a piece of content and providing it to the web editor for review

Reviewer and/or approver

Reviewers and approvers include subject matter experts, product or service managers, legal counsel, and other key stakeholders who are able to provide insight and information for the website. These individuals are typically "wrangled" by either the web editor or content strategist during the web content development process.

Web content is not a day-to-day responsibility for these folks, and it's likely to fall at the bottom of their to-do lists. It's very important to give reviewers and approvers a timely heads-up about when they'll be required to spend time with content drafts. It's all too common to turn over content with a request for review or approval by a certain date, only to have that date come and go without a response.

CASE STUDY STRIVING FOR CONSISTENCY IN SEO

James Mathewson was originally hired at IBM to focus on content-quality initiatives—creating a style guide and helping people follow it. But over the years, his role has evolved, and today, he is the global search strategy lead for IBM marketing (translation: he's really, really smart about SEO).

Improving content quality and search results

Using his combination of content and SEO skills, James has been able to help the IBM content team make huge strides in content quality and search results.

For example, on one project, they compared user research results about the kinds of search terms people used against an audit of actual content on the site. And they realized (through keyword research) that there were differences between the users' language and the company's terminology. As a result, the company developed content components specifically designed to bridge the gap.

Making SEO easy for content creators

In addition, James is working on several tools to help content creators incorporate SEO into their content more easily. With the help of Acrolinx, he's invented a plugin that alerts creators when their content is not optimized for search. He calls it a "spell checker on steroids." In addition to checking for SEO, the tool tells the creator when a keyword is inappropriate (either it is being used in another asset or it is not familiar to the audience), and suggests alternatives.

His next project is a database of user-friendly keywords, with features that will help govern keyword usage across the enterprise. The tool will help content creators choose appropriate keywords and manage how many times a keyword is used (so they don't create apparent duplicates and other bad user experiences).

James says, "Tooling makes following standards easy for page owners. We have an online style guide (which was recently published through IBM Press), but they have to check it regularly. They often don't have time or don't remember to check. If you build it into the tool, it's a drop-click operation … that helps us create relevant, high-value content for users."

When we talk about SEO people playing a role on the content team, James has it covered.

Should you hire or outsource?

Deciding whether to pay someone from the outside to create your content—or develop the in-house infrastructure to do it yourself—is a big decision. There's lots to consider.

Julie Vollenweider is the first point of contact for clients who contact Brain Traffic. She offers these guidelines to help you make your decision.

WHO SHOULD YOU HIRE?

OUTSOURCING IS BEST IF YOU:	IN-HOUSE RESOURCES ARE BEST IF YOU:
Want more time to focus on your brand/product/etc. core competencies (rather than content)	Are passionate about, and have time to devote to, content
Don't have budget and approval to hire an employee or a team	Have budget, time, understanding, and approval to hire at least one content employee
Have an unexpected or short-term need to focus on content	Have an ongoing need for content support

WHAT WILL YOU NEED TO DO?

OUTSOURCING REQUIRES:	IN-HOUSE RESOURCES REQUIRE:
A collaborative spirit	Alignment on the priority of content within your organization
Willingness to make a short-term investment	Empowerment to make and implement content decisions
Definition of content challenges/opportunities that need to be addressed	Definition of content roles and responsibilities
	Willingness and funds to make an ongoing investment in employee development, salaries, benefits, etc.

WHAT YOU CAN EXPECT?

WITH OUTSOURCING, YOU GET:	WITH IN-HOUSE RESOURCES, YOU GET:
Content expertise	Dedicated, full-time care and feeding for your content
External credibility and a fresh, objective perspective	Content expertise and deep organizational/product knowledge (over time)
Long-term cost savings	
Flexibility and scalability to match your changing content needs	

COMMITTEES AND COUNCILS: THE EXTENDED FAMILY

As we've discussed throughout the book, people throughout your organization, and beyond, have a big impact on your content. So, you need to involve your key stakeholders not only in the discovery and definition processes, but on an ongoing basis.

One way to do this is to form councils or committees—groups of informed stakeholders who can provide unique insight into content initiatives at regular intervals. Whether or not they have real decision-making power, the goal of these groups is to ensure your content or content strategy stays aligned with business goals and user needs.

Internal advisory council

With an internal advisory council, SMEs and other stakeholders are asked to weigh in on content activities and decisions. Although the content team is still ultimately responsible for making decisions and doing the work, having a council can be a valuable way to keep stakeholders informed, get people aligned, and understand perspectives from outside the content team.

Some of the most frequent council members are representatives from the following teams:

- Organizational leadership
- IT/site infrastructure
- Analytics/measurement
- Regional/country
- Marketing and offline promotions
- Procurement
- Legal/regulatory

The internal advisory council participates in high-level planning meetings, where the content team presents the content and discusses any relevant issues or problems. Topic areas include:

- Significant changes to the content strategy
- Policies and procedures

- Staffing and budget changes
- Sourcing/content acquisition plan
- Content measurement and feedback results
- Content retirement and removal

Web councils can become a permanent part of your strategy and planning cycle. As web governance expert Lisa Welchman notes, web councils can also be a temporary way to get people aligned and comfortable with new processes and policies. She says, "Sometimes, this is the council's most important function. I've seen web councils last for 12 to 18 months and then disband not because they were dysfunctional or ineffective, but because it had served its role as a catalyst for [collaboration] around the digital channel."*

Either way, internal alignment will always be critical to your content's success; a web council can help.

Audience advisory committee

Audience (user) advisory committees are a great way to get regular audience feedback on your content. These committees come in different sizes, but a team of 5–7 users is ideal. Often, non-profits use the advisory committee as a way to recognize volunteers who are already involved in the organization. For-profit businesses usually offer incentives for participation.

Ideally, the committee consists of volunteers representing key markets and audience groups (e.g., geographic areas and topic interests). They commit to staying on the committee for a specified length of time (usually a year), and are provided with training/insight on the organization's goals and objectives.

The committee acts as the users' voice. They:

- Provide insight into the user experience
- Evaluate current content
- Advise about content gaps
- Identify trends and opportunities in the user community

*http://www.welchmanpierpoint.com/blog/establishing-web-council

Good candidates can also be found by promoting the committee on the website itself, or sending an invitation to influential customers or bloggers. Aim for a mix of people who have different levels of involvement and history with the organization. And, be sure to report back to them on how their opinions were incorporated into your content work.

CASE STUDY DO YOU NEED MORE THAN ONE PERSON IN CHARGE?

When we talk about "centralized governance," people often assume we mean "one person who tells you what to do." That doesn't usually work, and it's especially tough when you're surrounded by subject matter experts with passionate ownership of their content. This is often the case in educational institutions; however, Normandale Community College in Bloomington, Minnesota, has developed a governance model to oversee the college's web strategy to minimize confusion and confrontation regarding web content.

Normandale originally formed a Web Content Advisory Committee in 2005. Two major problems arose: there were too many differing viewpoints to make quick and effective decisions; and having one committee chair responsible to implement web strategy decisions was unfair to the chair, time-consuming, and caused a bottleneck. As Director of Grant Development, Mary Krugerud remembers, "Our web initiatives moved painfully slowly."

Since then, a web governance structure has evolved that has proved to be extremely effective. Instead of just one person leading the charge, the new Web Strategy Committee has a leadership team that includes Mary as well as two other members: Normandale's Web Architect and the Dean of Marketing and Enrollment. As this year's committee chair, Mary has 25% of her time allocated to web duties. Mary brings her neutral role on campus, strong negotiating skills, and long history with the organization: ideal qualifications for the Chair.

The leadership team jokingly refers to their group as "The Triad," and they've had great success working together to keep web projects moving forward. They frequently lead independent workgroups to research new initiatives or other assignments. Best of all? Mary, as the Web Strategy Committee Chair, doesn't make governance decisions in isolation, so she is neither a bottleneck nor a lightning rod for criticism.

DESIGNING WORKFLOW AND GOVERNANCE PROCESSES

Having defined and assigned the appropriate roles for all the players, your job is to make sure they all work together as efficiently and productively as possible. To do that, you need a process.

When people think about the content development process, here's what they often imagine:

1. Concept ➤ 2. Create ➤ 3. Revise ➤ 4. Approve

In reality, content development usually looks a lot more like this:

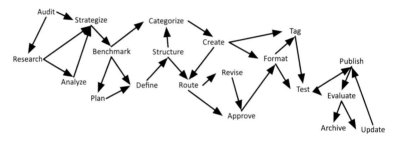

Once you realize the complexity of the content lifecycle, sitting down to identify or design your content processes can be pretty daunting. The secret to making content process design manageable is to break it down into smaller chunks. We often break the overall process down into these four areas of focus, each of which contain their own complex sub-processes:

- Create/source new content
- Maintain existing content
- Evaluate content effectiveness
- Govern strategies, plans, policies, and procedures

It's tempting to go down the list, check off these items one by one, and declare your content "officially done." **But, in reality, these activities are part of a continuous lifecycle that repeats and repeats and repeats.**

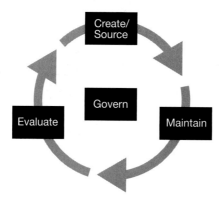

In the next few sections, we'll discuss things to consider while designing your process. For each of the four areas of focus, we'll cover:

- Common tasks
- Questions to consider
- Helpful tools

Note: Content processes, as discussed in this chapter, are independent of (although sometimes related to) content management system requirements and design. For more information, refer to Bob Boiko's book, *The Content Management Bible*, Chapter 33, "Designing Workflow and Staffing Models."

CREATING AND SOURCING CONTENT

Whether you're creating a whole new site or adding content to an existing site, there is a lot to do. Here are the most common ways new content is introduced to a website:

- **Original content creation:** Content is created in-house or by a vendor specifically for the use of the organization.
- **Curated or aggregated content:** Content is sourced from outside the organization and sometimes edited or annotated.
- **Content migration:** Content is moved from one content property or platform to another.

Common tasks

Often, creating and sourcing content includes the following tasks:

- Plan
- Create or source
- Route
- Revise
- Approve (including legal or regulatory)
- Add metadata
- Test
- Publish

Questions to ask yourself

While designing this stage of the process, you'll want to know:

- Where do requests for new content come from? Who receives them?
- Which business drivers (such as product launches, financial quarters, holidays, news, events) trigger requests for new content?
- Are there "emergency" content requests that arise? If so, what are they, why are they considered emergencies, and who can submit them?
- What information is most helpful to have before content work begins?
- Who is responsible for drafting/creating/selecting the content?
- Where do you get source material (for creation) or source content (curation/aggregation)?
- If content is curated or migrated, what kind of editorial work needs to happen?
- How are content drafts or selections routed between authors, approvers, and publishers?
- How are contracts negotiated for curated or aggregated content?
- What is a realistic timeframe to expect between a content request and publish date?
- If translation is required, how is it completed? How are translations assigned and approved?

- How does the content get published? Who does it? Does it have to be formatted in a specific way?
- Is there a staging environment, or do you just see the final product? Does the staging environment allow for changes or edits?

Helpful tools

Some tools that help manage this process include:

- **Editorial calendar:** A spreadsheet that captures future topic ideas, and schedules current content for publishing; includes authors, sources, and deadlines. (See "Tool Spotlight" below.)
- **Content requirements checklist:** A checklist of preferred content attributes used to determine if existing content or proposed future content is appropriate for your site.
- **Curation/aggregation checklist:** A checklist of steps required to select, contract, and publish third-party content.
- **Migration spreadsheet:** A spreadsheet that maps content from one channel, property, or process to another.

Tool spotlight: Editorial calendar

We're big fans of editorial calendars, and here's why: They help keep everyone on task and on the same page, which ultimately saves time, money, and heartache.

Creating your calendar

The first step toward a successful editorial calendar is defining why you're creating it. When you're defining the purpose for your calendar, be as specific as possible:

- Improve content quality or relevance.
- Integrate content across various channels/brands/business units.
- Fulfill user needs (by profile, lifecycle, or topics of interest).
- Align content with business goals/campaigns/events.
- Measure/record content success or value.
- Keep content creation on a manageable schedule.
- Allocate resources (human and budgetary) or justify resource needs.
- Manage all content creation/curation/maintenance activities.

When identifying purpose, don't forget to think about:

- Who is going to use the calendar and why?
- Are there multiple audiences that require different levels of information?
- How will it be shared/used?
- Who is going to maintain the calendar?
- How often will it be updated/shared?
- How will you know if the calendar is working?

Pick and prioritize calendar variables

Once you know the purpose, you can start choosing what to include on your calendar. There are literally hundreds of content-related variables that could be tracked on an editorial calendar. List all of the variables/data points you think are relevant to your calendar, then rank them in priority order.

It's tempting to include every tidbit of information you have, but in this case, less is usually more. Focus your calendar on the top priorities, and consider eliminating the bottom priorities to make your calendar easy to use and maintain.

For example, let's say you work for an organization that provides services to elementary school teachers. If you're creating an editorial calendar for your website, you might consider including the following variables:

1. Date (e.g., May 14)
2. Channel (e.g., website, print newsletter, Twitter)
3. Content element (e.g., home page article, newsletter sidebar, video)
4. Teacher profiles (e.g., new teacher, kindergarten teacher)
5. Teachers' events (e.g., National Teachers Association Convention)
6. Holidays and seasons (e.g., Christmas, autumn)
7. Hot topics (e.g., student testing, school security)
8. Content creator (e.g., web editor, Sue in marketing, third-party provider)
9. Content workflow step (e.g., schedule interviews, get outline approved, create content)
10. Budget (e.g., $5,000)

Depending on your priorities, your calendar will vary. For example, if the purpose of your calendar was to integrate all channels around user hot topics, your calendar might look like this:

Teacher's Aide, Inc. Editorial Calendar

Month:	September		
Week:	29-Aug	5-Sep	12-Se
Events:	National Teachers Association Convention		
Holidays:		US: Labor Day	
Hot Topics:	Convention highlights	Back to school/ Return from holidays	Preparing for flu season
Weekly web article series:	Guide to the convention, research spotlights	Assessing new student abilities	Safeguarding your classroom
Blog (2-3 x per week):	Convention highlights as they happen	Starting over with a new class: Teacher's stories	Lesson planning contigencies
Monthly print newsletter:	N/A	Setting goals for the year	N/A

Alternatively, if your calendar was mostly intended to manage resources and budgets, it might look like this:

Teacher's Aide, Inc. Editorial Calendar

29-Aug	Topic	Resource	Budget
Weekly web article series:	National Teachers' Association Convention: research spotlights	Freelance writer	$4,500
Blog (2-3 x per week):	Convention Highlights	Intern	$500
Monthly print newsletter:	N/A	N/A	N/A
5-Sep	Topic	Resource	Budget
Weekly web article series:	Back to School	Julie Jones (Product Manager)	65 hours
Blog (2-3 x per week):	Starting over with a new class: Teacher's stories	Intern editing user-generated content	$500
	Setting goals for the year	Sue Smith (Marketing Assistant)	20 hours

Editorial calendars don't have to be fancy or complicated. Whatever works for you, works.

MAINTAINING CONTENT

Once you deliver content anywhere online—particularly on your website—it's critically important that you maintain the content over time for accuracy, consistency, timeliness, and audience relevance. In other words, your content needs care and feeding. It won't take care of itself. Whether you're updating, archiving, or deleting content, you need a documented process for how maintenance gets done.

Common tasks

Often, maintaining content includes the following tasks:

- Plan
- Schedule
- Edit
- Route
- Revise
- Approve (including legal or regulatory)
- Add metadata
- Test
- Publish
- Retire/delete

Questions to ask yourself

While designing this stage of the process, find out:

- What are the triggers for content review, archiving, or removal?
- Are there regularly scheduled content updates? How often do they occur?
- Are there processes in place for on-the-fly updates and changes? When are these possible or acceptable?
- How are live content errors caught, tracked, and corrected?
- Who is in charge of performing, approving, and managing updates?
- What are the steps for publishing changes or edits?
- Where are source files stored for audio, graphics, video, and Flash-based elements? Who helps maintain these non-text elements?
- How is content archived or deleted? Manually, or is it an automated process within the CMS?
- If content is retired, does it need to be kept (for legal or other reasons) for any length of time? If so, where is it stored?
- What are the SEO implications of deleting or updating pages? Who manages that process?

Helpful tools

Some tools that help manage this process include:

- **Content inventory:** A spreadsheet to record and track all of your content, including title, author, topic, format, and more. (See *Chapter 5, Audit*, for examples.)

- **Content maintenance checklist**: A list of the criteria used to evaluate and prioritize content for maintenance.

- **Content maintenance log:** A CMS report or spreadsheet that provides dates for last update and next scheduled review.

EVALUATING CONTENT

Web content quality—and, ultimately, your business results and user satisfaction—benefits tremendously from ongoing "health and wellness" checkups: regularly-scheduled evaluations that provide the opportunity to add, improve, fix, or remove content. Checking in on your content consistently will help you see how content performs over time as business and user needs change. It also helps you understand how content activities change due to events like holidays or product launches.

Try to use a variety of measurement methods. When you use two or more methods, you'll get more well-rounded results. Some common methods include:

- **Qualitative assessments:** Review all of your audit based on specific quality criteria. (See *Chapter 5, Audit*.)

- **Analytics:** Use technology tools to collect data. (See *Chapter 6, Analysis*.)

- **User research and usability:** Ask the users directly what they want, or observe their behavior. (See *Chapter 6, Analysis*.)

- **External expert review:** Ask content experts or industry peers to review/rate content.

- **Internal expert review:** Get insights from knowledgeable people inside your organization, such as sales people or customer service reps.

- **Competitive comparison:** Measure direct competitors' content and your content on the same factors and compare. (See *Chapter 6, Analysis.*)
- **Operational evaluation:** Look at the costs (time, money, resources) associated with content creation and maintenance.

Any evaluation of content is somewhat subjective. Even the data gathered by analytics software needs subjective analysis. **The goal of the evaluation is to reduce uncertainty**. It provides your team (and your stakeholders) with enough information to make smart decisions about your content.

Common tasks
Often, evaluating content includes the following tasks:

- Define what content will be evaluated
- Define criteria by which the content will be evaluated
- Recruit reviewers (internal and external)
- Design evaluation
- Conduct evaluation
- Record results
- Analyze data
- Create report
- Communicate results

Questions to ask yourself
While designing this stage of the process, you'll want to know:

- What measurement techniques are most appropriate for our organization?
- Who is involved in the evaluation process?
- Are there other evaluation activities going on in the organization that you need to be aware of?
- How often should evaluations happen?
- Is there a set schedule for evaluations, or are they a reaction to business triggers?

- How will we track and share our results?

- Who do we need to share the results with? Do different people need different types of information?

- How do our results impact the other aspects of the content process (i.e., govern, create, and maintain)?

Helpful tools

Some tools that help manage this process include:

- **Qualitative audit spreadsheet and report:** Audit findings and data. (See *Chapter 5, Audit.*)

- **Measurement scorecard:** A spreadsheet or similar tool that helps stakeholders understand the results of your measurement findings. (See "Tool Spotlight" below.)

- **Measurement history:** An ongoing record of your measurement results (updated after each measurement activity) that provides information about how content performs over time.

Tool spotlight: Measurement scorecard

To get a clear picture of your content's health, you need to compile input from many sources and many different kinds of information. One effective way to do this is with a scorecarding system.

What is a scorecard?

A scorecard is a tool that brings together a variety of financial and non-financial metrics in a single, concise report. Score cards let you:

- Accommodate hundreds of metrics

- Combine financial results, analytics, user opinions, expert feedback, etc. into one report with quantifiable results

- Rank metrics by importance

- Summarize metrics results into clear performance scores that all members of your team can easily understand

How does it work?

To put together a scorecard:

- **Define what you want to measure and why (measurement factors).** Measurement factors need to be quantifiable.

- **Identify metrics for each factor.** Metrics can be sourced from many places, such as site analytics, expert opinions, or user testing.

- **Assign a target value to each metric.** What is the ideal "score" for the metric?

- **Assign a weight to each metric, if desired.** Sometimes, it's necessary to emphasize some metrics when calculating the score.

- **Measure content performance.** Record your results in the scorecard.

- **Calculate a score for each factor.** Combine the scores for all of the associated metrics to get a total score for the factor.

- **Calculate the total score for all factors.**

Like any measurement tool, scorecards work best when used regularly. Your first scorecard is the "baseline measurement." After that, each time you use your scorecard, you can see how the scores change and how much progress has been made.

Here's an example of what a scorecard might look like:

Teacher's Aide, Inc. Measurement Scorecard

Metrics (measurement factor)	Weight (x of 10)	Description	Measurement Results	Target Values	Score % of Target
Initial impact					
First impression	6	Score from quarterly user testing	82%	100%	82%
Clarity on what the content says	1	Score from quarterly user testing	95%	100%	95%
Visits to registration pages	4	From funnel report	13000	15000	87%
Total Score					87%
Depth of interest·					
Depth of visit	8	Average pages viewed per visit	4.81	5	96%
Time on site	3	Average time on site in seconds	300	450	67%
Traffic source	6	Traffic from bookmarks or typed URLS	37%	45%	82%

GOVERNING CONTENT

Most of this book has been about creating initial strategies and making sure plans are in place. Once that initial strategy is complete, you can ensure your strategies and plans are actionable and always up to date with *governance*. Governance will help you create, maintain, and update:

- **Core strategy:** The long-term direction of your content. (See *Chapter 7, Core.*)
- **Authority and ownership policies**: The people empowered to make decisions about content and content strategy.
- **Processes and procedures:** The way work gets done (See *this chapter*).
- **Plans and priorities:** The roadmaps for near-term initiatives and projects.
- **Content policies:** Non-optional rules or procedures the content team has to follow (for example, legal requirements).
- **Guidelines:** Generally understood sets of good practices that the content team ought to follow.

Common tasks

Often, governing content includes the following tasks:

- Review evaluation results
- Schedule workshops or meetings
- Conduct workshops or meetings
- Draft (the strategy, plan, procedure, guideline)
- Review
- Approve
- Communicate
- Collect feedback
- Update

Questions to ask yourself

While designing this stage of the process, you'll want to know:

- Who needs to participate in governance activities?
- How often should governance policies and procedures be updated?
- How are updates to style guides and legal requirements communicated?
- Which tools do you use (or wish you had) for content creation and updates?
- Are there different rules for different kinds of content (for example, a blog versus a product page)?

Helpful tools

Some tools that help manage this process include:

- **Style guide:** A guideline that ensures that content is consistent; used by anyone who creates, reviews, edits, or publishes content. (See "Tool Spotlight" below.)
- **Content planning and prioritization matrix:** A spreadsheet that helps you evaluate and prioritize content projects based on criteria drawn from your content strategy.
- **Meeting participation guide:** More than a meeting agenda, a document that lets participants in governance meetings know what's expected of them, and what to expect from the meeting.

Tool spotlight: Style guide

We've worked on hundreds of web content projects. And how many times has there been a style guide to reference for one of these projects? About six. Of those six style guides, sadly, only one of them was of any real use.

In her indispensable guide to writing web content, *Letting Go of the Words*, Ginny Redish devotes an entire chapter to creating what she calls an "organic" web content style guide. Here are some highlights:

- **Start small.** Let your style guide grow as issues and questions arise.
- **Focus on issues that keep coming up.** Your web writers likely have the same questions over and over. Make a decision, record it, and move on.

- **Put someone in charge.** The style guide isn't going to update itself. Make sure someone owns it and is accountable for its accuracy.

- **Put it online.** It's your most accessible, flexible, most cost-efficient option. In fact, a wiki might be a perfect option for your organization. Just make sure it has an owner to oversee its evolution.

Recommended style guidelines

Here are some examples of the types of information you may want to include in your style guide or style guide requirements:

- **Voice and tone guidelines.** Explain how you want your brand to sound, and how you want users to feel. (See *Chapter 6, Analysis.*)

- **Correct word usage.** This will vary among organizations. We recommend choosing specific terms and staying consistent (such as "team member" versus "employee").

- **Product trademark usage.** Clarify the need for special symbols and dates.

- **Web writing considerations.** Specifically, recommend how text links, labeling, metadata, and other repeating content elements should be documented, so that they remain consistent throughout your content.

- **Organization's choice of global style guide.** Rather than copying an entire grammar and usage manual into your content style guide, simply refer to the global style guide your organization decides upon, such as the *AP Stylebook* or *The Chicago Manual of Style.*

- **Web writing best practices.** This information may be a quick, one-page summary of tips on writing web content.

Make sure that the people who are creating, reviewing, and approving your content are all referring to the same playbook. You don't want to leave style open to individual interpretations.

DOCUMENTING YOUR PROCESSES

Whether you are creating a new process or changing an existing one, it helps to get things down on paper. That way, everyone involved can understand it and react to it. Processes are bound to change and evolve, so keeping your document(s) up to date is an ongoing task.

In *The Web Content Strategist's Bible*, Richard Sheffield offers these guidelines for documenting effective content processes:

1. Determine a starting point. (Author's note: Although we know content is a continuous lifecycle, the documentation needs a starting place. Common starting places are strategy development or a new content request.)

2. Figure out a logical place for the process to end. (Author's note: Some might say this is when content is delivered online; we'd argue it shouldn't end until content is archived or destroyed.)

3. Identify all players from beginning to end of the process. (Author's note: This should include not only content stakeholders, but also information architects, designers, developers, and anyone else who may need to weigh in on any content requests.)

4. Sketch the tasks.

5. Identify interaction patterns among players and tasks.

6. Allocate timeframes for tasks. (Author's note: These need to be REALITY-based, not impossibly ambitious.)

7. Identify notification patterns: who needs to know what at any given stage of the process.

8. Identify approval patterns.

9. Determine all the "what ifs" that may knock your process off its path.

10. Once all roles are identified, tasks are sketched, and notification and approval patterns are identified, examine your workflow to see if it can be simplified.

We provided a simple sketch of a workflow diagram in *Chapter 6, Analysis* (see page 81). There are literally thousands of other formats which vary widely in complexity and level of detail; ultimately, your needs and situation will shape a workflow diagram that's all your own.

MAKING IT HAPPEN

Once your content processes have been identified and designed, it's time to figure out a smart way to tell people about it and motivate them to adopt the process. There are a few things to consider, here:

Make people feel included

From the beginning, you've been asking people for their insights and input. Hopefully, you've incorporated their feedback into your process design. Therefore, they're already somewhat invested in this thing you're doing to make their lives easier. Be sure to keep them involved and informed as your content evolves.

Communicate the benefits

Old habits die hard. Don't expect to send a PDF of the process design to your coworkers and have everything running smoothly the next day. People do things the way they like to do them, regardless of whether it's the most efficient way. Introduce new workflow and governance processes by clearly communicating the benefits—not only to the organization as a whole, but to the individuals who will be responsible for making the overall effort a success.

Give it time

People will need some time to adapt to a new process, especially if you're simultaneously teaching them how to use a new CMS. Identify your success measures. Track usage. Celebrate short-term wins. Make sure people are clearly seeing the end-product benefits: that content is more accurate, more consistent, more in line with the vision of what it should be.

LOOK WHAT YOU'VE DONE

Okay. We're nine chapters in. Let's review.

You've learned about what content strategy is and why you need it. You've done a deep-dive analysis of your content and the things that impact it. You've created a core strategy and made smart decisions about substance, structure, workflow, and governance. You've aligned the troops again and again.

Who's awesome? You're awesome. High fives.

Of course, there's more to success than methodology. The real world awaits …

SUCCESS

· ·

Are you itching to save the world with your newfound content strategy superpowers? Before you embark, there are a few things you should know.

10 PERSUASION

YOU ARE SO TOTALLY AMPED. You know what content strategy is and why it's important. You know what to do, and you're ready for action. So, here's the big question: How can you persuade clients or colleagues to take on a content strategy project?

Whether you're a consultant or working inside an organization, making the case for content strategy can feel like an uphill battle. Not only do you have to get people interested in content, but you need to get them to participate in—and pay for—content strategy work. So bothersome.

In this chapter, we'll talk about how to:

- Start the conversation.
- Tell a good story.
- Pitch your project.
- Get the budget.

You can do this. We promise.

START THE CONVERSATION

When you're starting out, the goal is to get as many people excited about content strategy as possible. The more people understand about the value of content strategy, the more willing they'll be to invest in it. There are a couple ways to go about it.

BANG THE DRUM

Start making lots of noise about content strategy. Tell everyone you know what content strategy is, and why they should care. Give talks and hold workshops about it. Leave your copy of this book on your boss's desk. Write a blog or an email, and forward it to your clients and colleagues.

One hint, though. Before you march into the CEO's office with a proposal of what you're going to do and when, practice on some people who you know are sympathetic to your cause and can help refine your ideas.

GO STEALTH

During a 2011 presentation at Confab: The Content Strategy Conference, Michael Fienen (Director of Web Marketing, Pittsburg State University) reminded the audience, "People in organizations will often look at content strategy as just more work." He advocates for "stealth content strategy"—in other words, don't formalize or advertise your efforts. Casually mention—and keep mentioning—content issues.

Or, if you're already a content professional, steer conversations toward more strategic activities. Look for opportunities to forward people content strategy tools (like checklists or editorial calendars), articles, or blog posts—as if you stumbled across them and thought they might be useful. Hide the zucchini in the brownies. Wear dark sunglasses and hide behind people's monitors. Oh, wait. Don't do that. Just try to ease people into the conversation slowly.

YOU'VE GOT TO START SOMEWHERE

How you start the conversation depends on the organization, the person you're talking to, your personality, and the urgency of your content problems. Whether you quietly take the stealth approach or start waving the content strategy flag, the important thing is to take action.

TELL A GOOD STORY

The absolutely most effective way to win support is to tailor your message
to each audience. Don't just write generic emails about the topic of content
strategy and blast them out to all your colleagues. Put content strategy in
the context of their world—why should they care, and what will they get
out of it? Think about what the individual or group wants (or is supposed)
to accomplish. What projects are their priorities? Why? What's in their
way? What are the things keeping them up at night? (You can probably get
this out over coffee. Or happy hour.) Then, working backwards, build a
case around their worst pain points or biggest opportunities. Focus on how
content strategy will specifically help them get wins where they need to.
Make your constant subliminal message be, "When we do this work, you
will come out looking like a rock star."

(By the way, if someone has given you this book to help build their case for
content strategy … say "yes." Because when the two of you do this work,
both of you will come out looking like rock stars. Or ninjas. Or both!)

PITCH YOUR PROJECT

When you have people's attention, it's time to take things to the next level:
proposing a specific project. Although the exact conversation you have is
audience-specific, there are several high-level themes you can use.

"OUR USERS DESERVE BETTER CONTENT"

If good user experience is a value the team shares, appeal to their inclina-
tion to do right by their audiences. After all … it's impossible to design a
good user experience with bad content.

Provide examples of how content can assist—and fail—the users. Haul
out those particularly cringe-worthy pieces of their content if you have
to. Scour user testing and surveys for proof. Or, if you're really lucky, get
some content-specific user testing on the docket—even if it's part of a
bigger study.

Good content will increase audience trust and engagement, which in turn will help your bottom line. Keep reminding your stakeholders that people don't come to your website for visual appeal or complex technical features: They come for the content.

"CONTENT STRATEGY WILL MAKE US MORE EFFICIENT"

When in doubt, lead with workflow. Better content is a noble cause, but content quality may seem like a subjective goal to some. Almost everyone, however, can agree that inefficiencies are no good. Getting good processes in place simplifies everyone's lives, saves time and money, and is conducive to workplace sanity.

Just point out how screwed up the content process really is. Highlight:

- **Overlaps and gaps:** "Does the marketing team really need to review content three times to ensure brand consistency ... or could a joint content style guide help?"

- **Impacts to the bottom line:** "Everyone calls our customer service phone number instead of getting the info on the website. If we could make the website content more clear, we could save lots of cash in call center staffing."

- **Errors and inconsistencies:** "This content got passed around so much, we lost track of who was editing what. Now it contradicts most of the pages that link to it."

- **Embarrassing misses:** "The 'coming soon' link on our home page is for a product that launched two months ago. Do we even know whose job it is to change that?'"

"OUR COMPETITORS ARE WINNING"

You know from *Chapter 6, Analysis* that just because your competitors are doing something, doesn't mean you should. But if your website content was created in 1998 and your competitor has a shiny new site that's a serious threat, you might have to play the competitor card.

The "everyone else is doing content strategy" argument can have a silly amount of power. Nothing gets people riled up like fighting against a common enemy. Just be sure to invest time on a comprehensive, content-focused competitive review, so you can concentrate on competitive advantage, not specific features or tactics.

"THE NUMBERS SAY IT ALL"

Business is, by and large, a numbers game. So, quantifying content strategy—whether its opportunity or potential loss—can make a huge impact. Use the results of your audit, site traffic statistics, and other sources to tabulate *numbers* that support your cause:

- Work with your sales or customer service teams to identify the number of incoming comments or calls that could have been addressed with better content. Even better, couple this with the average cost of an incoming call to show how much money can be saved.

- Find specific pain points you can measure that force stakeholders to face the ugly truth about the condition of their online content:
  - Number of mistakes or inaccuracies found in the content
  - Percentage of outdated or inaccurate content
  - Number of pages that have virtually no traffic … or none at all
  - Number of pages or sections that have no identifiable owners

- Follow up your "scary" numbers with the percentage of your audience that use online sources, especially in making decisions that impact your business. Emphasize the fact that your audience isn't coming to your website for fancy design, social media widgets, or a CMS bloated with "nice to have" features: they're coming for the content.

Get the details, do some projections, and use numbers to set up the dire situation and hero opportunity.

GET THE BUDGET

Getting people interested in content strategy is one thing. Getting them to invest in a content strategy project is totally different. Whether you are an outside consultant with a proposal, or an insider requesting budget—you need to have a plan.

OPTION 1: START SMALL

If content strategy is new to the organization, a terrific option is to start with a "pilot" project to help you prove the value of content strategy. If your project goes well, it's much easier to get a bigger budget next time. Focus on getting measurement and metrics to keep proving your case. Get some really solid numbers. Share the results with anyone and everyone.

In her blog post, "The Inside Job," Brain Traffic's Christine Benson advises:

> Find low visibility content with high potential. People often have strong opinions about the home page and main section pages. These content hot spots can be difficult starting points until you have some success stories to back you up. Look for things that have high potential for customer engagement, but usually get ignored. Support content like help sections, customer service pages, or error messages are good candidates.*

Something to keep in mind: Starting small can be a great way to give people a taste of content strategy success, but there can be disadvantages, too. People may get the impression that future content strategy activities will be "cheap" like the initial investment. Or, they might think it's okay to do lots of little projects, instead of doing a more all-inclusive strategy. These misperceptions are easily managed, as long as you set expectations appropriately from the start. Just be sure to keep communicating about the bigger picture to stakeholders throughout the project.

OPTION 2: GO BIG

If you want to make a big impact immediately, then go ahead. Propose a big project. Propose a whole website content redesign. Address social media content from top-to-bottom. Suggest an entire integrated cross-channel web content strategy.

While this approach may seem scary (or nuts), there are definite advantages to going for the whole enchilada. Explain to your client or team that doing it right the first time is a money saver/maker in the long run. Content is an investment. Plain and simple.

---

*http://blog.braintraffic.com/2011/07/the-inside-job-getting-started/

It's like a house remodeling project. If you can have a contractor come in, bid it out, do it all at once … you will get a big bill. But, if you had a contractor come in 10 times, you'll get several smaller bills that will add up quickly.

A FEW IMPORTANT HINTS

Regardless of the size of the project you're proposing, when you ask for money, we encourage you to:

- **Ask in person.** Don't just email a proposal. Sit in the room and have a discussion (even if you feel uncomfortable). Or, if you can't be there in person, schedule a phone call. That way, your stakeholder can ask questions, and you can clarify the finer points. A slight change in wording or scope can make or break your case

- **Know your current budget**. If you're an employee or a consultant with an existing client relationship, take a good look at your current budget. Make sure you know what you can—and can't—do with the funds you have today. Show how previous funds were put to good use, and be prepared to answer questions about why you need more. They'll ask.

- **Understand the organization's fiscal year**. If you understand the organization's budgeting, planning, and reporting schedule, you can often target good times to ask for money. During the annual planning process? Good idea. At the end of the year, when people need to spend their remaining cash or lose it? A very, very good idea. Don't be afraid to ask your client or boss straight-out when the optimal times are.

AND IF THERE IS NO BUDGET?

So you didn't get the cash this time … or there was never any cash to be had. Don't be discouraged. Chances are, you can still do something. If you're an internal employee, comb through your existing budget again. What can get sacrificed? Can another department help?

No matter what, keep building your case for content strategy, slowly but surely. Ask your stakeholders what's keeping them from supporting the project. What would it take to get this project or another similar one funded? Is there somebody else you need to talk to? Be on the lookout for like-minded colleagues who can help you achieve some first steps. Be patient. It'll be worth it.

A NOTE TO THE BIGWIGS

Yes. You there. With the budget.

If we haven't quite made the case for the incredible impact content strategy can have on your organization's performance and bottom line, then at least allow us to encourage you to give content strategy a chance to show you a few small wins.

If you give somebody on your team the support and authority to dig deeply into your web content and the ecosystems in which it lives, you will get answers to questions you didn't even know you had. You'll be presented with recommendations and solutions that will improve your content quality, deliver on your online users' expectations, and support your core business objectives.

If you force your content people into narrowly defined roles that essentially relegate them to a life of order-taking and production, you will never realize an iota of the benefits content strategy can offer.

Have their back, and help them make their case. Believe us when we tell you: Your content people have been waiting for the opportunity to step up to the plate for a long, long time. Give them the chance, and they'll deliver for your business in spades.

NOW, REMEMBER

As of right now, you're a salesperson. No more sitting in the corner and complaining about how no one pays any attention to the content. Get out there and get pitching!

p.s. This book is a very good size and thickness for smacking on the table to emphasize your point. Or whacking someone in the back of the head. Or killing a wasp. Regardless, wield it as your weapon. "Someone published a book on content strategy, and the book is red, and that means EMERGENCY and STOP, so it must be very important!" It has worked for others. It can work for you.

p.p.s. You didn't hear any of this from us.

ADVOCACY

NO MATTER WHO YOU ARE—practitioner, executive, manager, student, or curious bystander—it's within your power to assume responsibility for improving the content you create and manage.

Don't worry. We're not going to tell you to buy a tour bus and hit the road with a Content Strategy Jamboree ... although we certainly wouldn't discourage it. There are all sorts of ways you can advocate for content strategy, in the workplace or out in the world. You can:

- Talk straight, not tech.
- Champion "content always."
- Take to the streets.

TALK STRAIGHT, NOT TECH

One inevitable challenge with the topic of content strategy—or any evolving discipline, really—is finding the right words to explain what it is and why it matters. Whether you're a rookie or an old pro, there's no getting around it: You'll have to have this conversation over and over—with clients, with colleagues, or with your aunt at Thanksgiving who's not going to let you get away with saying, "Oh, you know. I do Web stuff."

Here's a little demonstration of what *not* to do:

Person : "So! What do you do?"

You: "I'm a content strategist."

Person: "Oh! What does that mean?"

You: "In many companies, the content lifecycle is totally undefined and ignored. Content is constantly getting produced in silos, and no one is fully accountable for its governance. And the problem is just getting worse, because no one understands that content requires strategic consideration and dedicated resources. So I analyze, strategize, and implement solutions that help businesses realize their goals while ensuring users are able to successfully meet their objectives."

Person: "I think I'm getting a call on my cell." [runs away, screaming]

This explanation consists of terms that, while perfectly familiar to the practiced content strategist, have the potential to immediately alienate someone who may, in fact, need help with exactly what you do. In general, unfamiliar words freak people out. Front-loading the conversation with insider terminology turns content into a hot potato. It doesn't work. Also, you will never be invited to parties again.

Here's a simpler way this go could down:

Person: "So! What do you do?"

You: "I'm a content strategist."

Person: "Oh! What does that mean?"

You: "You know how, on lots of the websites you go to, most of the information is hard to find, or inconsistent, or totally irrelevant, or just really bad?"

Person: "Yes, it is! In fact, my own company's site is straight-up embarrassing. I'm so frustrated that no one is fixing it."

You: "That's what I do. I fix it."

Person: "And how might I acquire some of this so-called 'content strategy'? Because I happen to be the CEO of this company, and we have millions of dollars that I would like to pay you as soon as possible."

Plain English is powerful, isn't it? Also, note that this conversation is actually a place where introducing content strategy *for the Web* makes perfect sense. Commiserating about how websites suck is an activity everyone enjoys. And why are websites so bad? The content. Boom! You're in.

At this point, you have an opening to explain basic principles using constraints (website vs. company-wide content lifecycle) that make it seem achievable. Furthermore, when you're talking to clients and colleagues, this initial exchange ends up being a very sensible, non-scary starting point for the much larger discussion that inevitably arises: "This isn't just about our website. This is about the way content moves throughout our organization and the way we manage our content assets."

CHAMPION "CONTENT ALWAYS"

Now and then, someone will post an especially egregious example of "lorem ipsum" placeholder text that was never removed from the final product. For example:

Or:

Hahahaha. Ahem.

While no one loves lorem ipsum fails more than we do, this all-too-common oversight has caused many within the design and content communities to take up the cry of "content first!"—which, in this context, translates to "get the copy first, then design for it." Most designers will tell you that this is what they want to do, and they've been asking for content first their entire careers. Unfortunately, they rarely have control over when the content hits their inbox; this, of course, is a problem. And if designers always waited for real content, they might have to put projects on hold for years. (Some of them do.)

So, try to look at it this way, instead: "content first" isn't "copy first." It's about considering content—its impact factors, goals, and lifecycle—from the very beginning of the design process.

Actually, now that we think about it...

This hits it. If there's anything we've learned so far, it's that content must be considered throughout and beyond any design and development project, no matter what the plan or platform is. So, not "content first." Content *always*.

Facebook content strategist Tiffani Jones Brown wrote about this shift in thinking on her blog, in a post titled, "Toward a Content-Driven Design Process":

> One of the biggest and best side effects of content strategy's activism is that it's encouraging agencies to reorder their design process. It's no longer: discovery, information architecture, design, templates, and development. Instead, we're doing: content strategy, information architecture, web writing, content production, design, templates, and development—or some version of this.
>
> The important thing is, we're starting to think about content, early on. From a designer's perspective, this means we no longer begin projects by evaluating the design of a site; we start by evaluating what's **on** it. Text, videos, etc. Do they make sense? Do they achieve the intended effect? Are they interesting?
>
> … It would be silly to think that every agency is going to upend its process in the name of content strategy. For most agencies, I smell a rapprochement, not a revolution: IAs, designers, and art directors will learn or enhance their content strategy skills.*

And who doesn't love a good rapprochement?

TAKE TO THE STREETS

Raise your right hand. Go on, do it.

Now read this aloud:

"I hereby swear never, ever, ever to say the words, 'I can't blog or speak at conferences or write articles or give a presentation to my boss or tweet or speak up at meetings because I don't have anything interesting to say.'"

Once more. WITH FEELING.

---

*http://thingsthatarebrown.com/blog/2010/05/toward-a-content-driven-design-process/

When you work at a job day in and day out, you tend to forget that there are many, many other people out there who don't know what it is that you do … or that do what you do and need ideas about how to do it differently, or better.

You think you don't have anything to talk about only because the stuff you do seems so dang *obvious* and *ordinary*. But it only seems that way to you. There are folks who would very much like for you to explain to them what you do, why you do it, and what you're discovering along the way.

After all, you want to know what *they're* up to, too, don't you?

Be brave, people. Get out there and do something.

BLOG IT UP

Ever heard of WordPress? How about TypePad? Tumblr? Blogger? Yes. You have. This means you can have a blog—a free one, at that.

Go take a look at some of the blogs listed below. Some of these folks have been writing about content strategy for years; some of them just started blogs within the last few months. Regardless, every single one of them is contributing to how the field evolves, not to mention helping out their fellow content strategists with new insights and how-to tools.

> Ian Alexander – eatmedia.net/blog
>
> Rahel Bailie – intentionaldesign.ca
>
> Clinton Forry – content-ment.com
>
> Matthew Grocki – grassfedcontent.wordpress.com
>
> Richard Ingram – richardingram.co.uk
>
> Colleen Jones – leenjones.com
>
> Jonathan Kahn – lucidplot.com
>
> Corey Vilhauer – eatingelephant.com
>
> Sara Wachter-Boettcher – endlesslycontent.com

GET ONSTAGE

If the idea of speaking in public makes you want to throw up, please skip to the following section.

If you look forward to giving presentations at your company, or have dabbled in public speaking before, or even if you have a little theater experience, you might try your hand at giving a presentation about content strategy. Not only is it super helpful to your audience, it's also a terrific way for you to work at shaping your own perspectives, no matter what the focus of your presentation may be.

Need some inspiration? Go to slideshare.net, search for "content strategy" (natch), and check out the dozens of decks posted there. Know that these presentations were given by expert and novice speakers alike. Slideshare is also a great place to gather ideas about where you might find opportunities to present (check the title slide for the name of the meeting or conference). If nothing else, start with your team or your clients.

COLLECT AND SHARE GOOD STUFF

If you spend time online learning about content strategy—or go to a conference, or read a book (ahem), or otherwise experience something about content strategy—you have the option to share that resource or experience with others. It's likely you're already doing this somewhere with other topics or objects—Facebook, Twitter, Etsy, Flickr, and Tumblr, to name a few. Why not pick a place and do this with content strategy resources? It's low risk, and it doesn't require a big time commitment. People will love you for it.

ALL RIGHT, THEN. NO EXCUSES.

Because you have read this book, you have the opportunity—nay, the obligation!—to spread the word about this awesome thing called "content strategy." When it comes to advocacy, there's something for everyone.

What will *you* do?

12 HERO

WHENEVER WE TEACH WORKSHOPS, there are two things we hear from people over and over again.

The first is this:

> We're still doing content wrong in our company, and I'm really embarrassed about it.

Even if these aren't the exact words attendees use, it's the message they're sending loud and clear every time they raise their hand to ask a question. "Sorry my company is so behind the curve, but …" or "I realize everyone else knows what they're doing, but …"

The thing is, there are very, very few organizations that actually have their acts together when it comes to content. So, if you're sitting in a content strategy workshop, you're actually ahead of the game. You're not late to the party. The content strategy conversation has only begun.

Here's the second thing people say:

> This is hard.

Well, HELL YES, it's hard. You're not going to leave a workshop or a one-hour talk and go back to your company and suddenly find yourself with funding and staff and group hugs.

So what you need, dear friend, is friends. Content strategy friends. There are so many of them out there, and they're just as smart and curious as you are. (For some reason, they're pretty funny, too.)

Here's what you can do.

GET IN A GROUP

Whether you actively participate or just lurk in the shadows, there are a few amazing, active online groups to check out. Two of our favorites:

Content Strategy Google Group:
http://groups.google.com/group/contentstrategy

LinkedIn Content Strategy Group:
http://www.linkedin.com/groups/Content-Strategy-1879338

FOLLOW THE HASHTAG

If you're a tweeter, follow #contentstrategy on Twitter.com for the best curated content strategy content around.

GO TO—OR START—A MEETUP

Meetup.com is a great website that allows absolutely anyone to schedule an event and open it up to all interested parties. Meetup.com has been absolutely essential in helping content-loving folks find each other in cities around the world. Some content strategy meetups have started with three people and grown to three hundred in less than a year!

How can you find one of these magical events? It's easy. Go here:

http://content-strategy.meetup.com

Enter your ZIP code to see if there's one in your area. If there is, then register for the next one and go! Meet friends. Learn things. Be happy.

If there's not, then start one. Yes. Looking at you. Just follow the instructions, post your link wherever you can (those groups we mentioned would be great places), and see what happens. It's super simple, and it's low risk:

If at least one person shows up, then at least you can enjoy a drink together while venting about how no one at your company gets content except for you.

> Bonus: If you do start a Meetup, find Kristina (@halvorson) on Twitter and let her know. She'll help you advertise it. And don't forget to use the #contentstrategy hashtag wherever you can!

SHARE THE DREAM

Once you connect with all of these fellow content lovers, ask them to keep reminding you of the following:

Content is a huge, pain-in-the-butt, expensive, out-of-control problem. And, as with any big, messy problem, getting to a solution is going to take time.

Be. Patient.

Creating a smart content strategy means research and reflection, trial and error. And selling it to The Powers That Be—winning attention, approval, and resources—may take even longer. And you know what? That's okay. You have time. (Remember: It's only the Internet.)

Along the way, keep reminding everyone (including yourself) of the benefits:

- More lasting website improvements
- Huge savings on content licensing
- Streamlined, more efficient workflow
- Vastly improved user experiences
- New types of cross-team collaborations
- More consistency in multi-platform content
- Better realization of overall business goals

These are the things you get when you put content strategy to work for your organization. What's not to love?

AND THAT ABOUT COVERS IT

Congratulations! Because you have now read *Content Strategy for the Web*, we hereby anoint you as a member of The Order of People Who Have Read Content Strategy for the Web. As a member of TOOPWHRCSFTW, it's now your job to get out there and figure out what can be done to improve the way you and your clients or colleagues create, deliver, and govern your web content. With your help, we can all consider content at the strategic level, so we can start to deliver the right stuff: content that matters, both to our audiences and to our bottom line.

So, get busy! There's a whole lot of content out there in the world that needs your help. Be brave. Be informed. Be awesome. Be the hero you were born to be.

All of us here at TOOPWHRCSFTW wish you well as you begin your quest for content success. Now, go put on your cape and get to it. We're counting on you!

CONTENT STRATEGY READING LIST

Content Strategy at Work: Real-world Stories to Strengthen Every Interactive Project
by Margot Bloomstein

Content Management Bible
by Bob Boiko

Communicating Design: Developing Web Site Documentation for Design and Planning
by Dan Brown

The Necessary Art of Persuasion
by Jay A. Conger

The Elements of User Experience
by Jesse James Garrett

Content Rules
by Ann Handley and C. C. Chapman

The Accidental Taxonomist
by Heather Hedden

Clout: The Art and Science of Influential Web Content
by Colleen Jones

The Elements of Content Strategy
by Erin Kissane

Don't Make Me Think
by Steve Krug

Responsive Web Design
by Ethan Marcotte

Audience, Relevance, and Search: Targeting Web Audiences with Relevant Content
by James Mathewson, Frank Donatone, Cynthia Fishel

Killer Web Content: Make the Sale, Deliver the Service, Build the Brand
by Gerry McGovern

Information Architecture for the World Wide Web
by Peter Morville & Louis Rosenfeld

Letting Go of the Words
by Ginny Redish

Managing Enterprise Content: A Unified Content Strategy, second edition
by Ann Rockley and Charles Cooper

Designing for Emotion
by Aarron Walter

What Is Strategy and Does It Matter
by Richard Whittington

The Paradox of Choice: Why More Is Less
by Barry Schwartz

The Web Content Strategist's Bible: A Complete Guide to a New and Lucrative Career for Writers of All Kinds
by Richard Sheffield

Building Findable Websites: Web Standards, SEO, and Beyond
by Aarron Walter

Mobile First
by Luke Wroblewski

ACKNOWLEDGMENTS

Every acknowledgments page starts off with how it's impossible to write a book alone, and there's very good reason for that: it's SO TRUE. So here's where we extend our thanks to the small army of contributing individuals and teams who helped bring the second edition of *Content Strategy for the Web* to life.

Our deepest thanks to…

Tenessa Gemelke, editor extraordinaire. Because of your tireless efforts, elegant diplomacy, and ruthless optimism, this book is a reality. We were so lucky to have you on this project, and we can't thank you enough for your work. Also, nice outfit.

The team at Brain Traffic, whose groundbreaking work has informed much of what we've included in this second edition. You exceed our expectations every day. You inspire and delight us. Thanks for working here. We love your faces.

The best readers ever: Christine Anameier, Christine Benson, Meghan Casey, Tenessa Gemelke, Colleen Jones, Erin Kissane, Chris LaVictoire Mahai, Claire Rasmussen, Lee Thomas, and Julie Vollenweider. Thank you for whipping our chapter drafts into shape with your insightful feedback.

The people who contributed the lovely images and graphics herein: Christine Benson, Shelly Bowen, Kevin Cornell, and Sean Tubridy.

The case study participants, who have brought content strategy to life: Laura Blaydon, Dominique Bohn, Matt Crawford, Carrie Dennison, Lynne Figg, Kate Kiefer, Erika Knudson, Mary Krugerud, James Mathewson, Blair Neufeld, Rebecca Salerno, and Shelly Wilson.

Michael Nolan, our New Riders acquisitions editor. Thanks for (strongly) encouraging a second edition.

Nancy Aldrich-Ruenzel, vice-president of Pearson Technology Group and publisher at Peachpit Publishing, who first opened the door for this book to be published.

Margaret Anderson, Cory Borman, and the entire New Riders team.

All those who made invaluable contributions to the first edition of *Content Strategy for the Web*. No first edition, no second edition; thank you for making this book possible: Ian Alexander, Rahel Bailie, Margot Bloomstein, Jennifer Bohmbach, Bob Boiko, Jennifer Bove, Shelly Bowen, Craig Bromberg, Paul Ford, Maggie Fox, Colleen Jones, Jonathan Kahn, Rachel Lovinger, Erin Malone, Jeffrey MacIntyre, James Mathewson, Mark McCormick, Gerry McGovern, Elena Melendy, Chris Moritz, Clare O'Brien, Joe Pulizzi, Lou Rosenfeld, Dan Saffer, Richard Sheffield, Amber Simmons, Daniel Souza, Molly Wright Steenson, Krista Stevens, Lisa Welchman, Carolyn Wood, and the participants of the 2009 Content Strategy Consortium.

Also, Melissa says...

A special thanks to my career mentors (so far): Don Johnson and Jeff Iseminger, for getting me started; Cindy Larson, for showing me how to be a "business woman"; Brenda Kienan and Sole, for countless hours collaborating; Lisa Brezonik, for the reality checks; and Chris LaVictoire Mahai, for teaching me a great many things about strategy and success.

I'd also like to give a shout out to all of the incredible teams I've worked on during the last few decades. Specifically, I'd like to thank my friends from KeyTech/AisleFive/Aveus—the early internet agency(ies?) where I "grew up". (We turned out pretty well for web geeks.) And, to the Brain Traffic team: You keep me growing and learning new things every day; thanks for all of your brilliance, hard work, humor, and moral support on this project and always.

To Julie Vollenweider and Kristina Halvorson: Running a business isn't always easy, but it is so worthwhile. I'm proud to be a part of the "triangle." Thanks for all you do.

Most of all, thanks to my family, who give me substance, structure, and—sometimes—a little governance. My parents, Liz and Dick, who always believe in me no matter what; Matt, who gives me courage when needed; Marcie and Elsa, who watch from afar; and Beatrice, my very best girl. Thank you for your patience and support. I love all of you more than I can say.

And finally, Kristina says…

I'm not exaggerating when I say that I owe my career and personal sanity to these extraordinary individuals:

Liz Danzico, Peter Merholz, Jared Spool, and Jeffrey Zeldman, who opened doors. I can trace nearly every opportunity I have today back to your initial actions and support. Thank you, thank you.

Lisa Brezonik, Ann Handley, Ginny Redish, Ann Rockley, Lou Rosenfeld, and Dan Roam, who lead by example. Thank you for inspiring me professionally and personally.

Erika Hall, Jeremy Keith, Ethan Marcotte, Eric Meyer, Mike Monteiro, Sarah Parmenter, Jason Santa Maria, Nicole Sullivan, Aarron Walter, and Luke Wroblewski. You are the people who make the Web go.

Mandy Brown, Elise Diedrich, Laura Funke, Symantha Huhn, Erin Kissane, Rachael Marret, Karen McGrane, Kate McRoberts, Melissa Rach, Julie Vollenweider, and Christine Weeks. Thanks for knowing everything about me and being my friends anyway.

My parents, who—along with my extended family—support me in everything I do. Thanks for rolling with it.

And finally, Gus and Ingrid, who are the smartest, funniest, toughest, sweetest creatures alive. It's such an honor to be your mom. I love you infinity.

ABOUT THE AUTHORS

Kristina Halvorson is widely recognized as the industry's leading advocate for content strategy. She is the CEO and founder of Brain Traffic; the founder of Confab, the content strategy conference; and the host of Content Talks, a 5by5 podcast. She is a celebrated speaker on content strategy—her humorous, lively talks are regularly top-rated at conferences all over the world. She lives in St. Paul, Minnesota with her two children.

Melissa Rach is co-founder of Dialog Studios (dialogstudios. com) a content-focused business consultancy. She was previously vice president of content strategy at Brain Traffic. In addition to helping clients solve tough content problems, she speaks and writes regularly about strategy, content processes, and content's impact on business. Her content methodologies have been taught by universities nationwide and recognized in books and blogs for more than a decade. Melissa lives in Minneapolis with her family and names her pets after punctuation marks.

Visit http://www.contentstrategy.com to get in touch with the authors.

ABOUT BRAIN TRAFFIC

Brain Traffic collaborates with organizations to create and implement content strategies for projects and enterprises. Its renowned consulting team is credited with developing many recognized industry best practices. Brain Traffic was founded in 2005 and is headquartered in Minneapolis, Minnesota.

INDEX